SINCLAIR

THE SCOTLAND YARD PUZZLE BOOK

HEADLINE

The right of Sinclair McKay to be identified as the Author of
the Work has been asserted by him in accordance with the
Copyright, Designs and Patents Act 1988.

First published in 2019
by HEADLINE PUBLISHING GROUP

5

Cataloguing in Publication Data is available from the British Library

Trade paperback ISBN 978 1 4722 5833 5
Ebook ISBN 978 1 4722 5832 8

'Scotland Yard ' registered trademark of the Mayor's Office of Policing and Crime.

Designed by Couper Street Type Co.
Printed and bound in Great Britain by
Clays Ltd, Elcograf S.p.A.

Headline's policy is to use papers that are natural, renewable and recyclable products and
made from wood grown in sustainable forests. The logging and manufacturing processes are
expected to conform to the environmental regulations of the country of origin.

HEADLINE PUBLISHING GROUP
An Hachette UK Company
Carmelite House
50 Victoria Embankment
London EC4 0DZ

www.headline.co.uk
www.hachette.co.uk

CONTENTS

INTRODUCTION

Ask anyone in Moscow, Beijing or New York what the name Scotland Yard evokes and the chances are that their responses will be the same: foggy streets, a stout constable with a blue helmet and perhaps a rain cape, piercing police whistles, and detectives in thick overcoats instantly uncovering tiny but vital case-cracking clues.

This ought, for the British, to be a source of national pride. Just how many police forces around the world attract tourists who will queue to have their photo taken beneath the headquarters' signs? New Scotland Yard – and its 1970s vintage revolving sign – attracts countless visitors daily. Tourists ask for selfies with officers going in and out of the building. The institution has an unshakeable grip on the global imagination. This is partly because of the wealth of fiction set in and around the Yard – atmospheric novels, lovingly detailed period films – but it is also because the Yard's real history is a frequently dazzling narrative of ingenuity and wild inventiveness in the face of seemingly insoluble crimes. It is an enduringly human institution that has taken on, and beaten, some of the most charismatically wicked criminals the world has ever seen.

The image of the Scotland Yard detective is not the same as the other-worldly, lateral portrayals of Conan Doyle's Sherlock Holmes. The Yard's moments of inspiration are quieter, the method grittier and more dogged. Unlike Holmes, our real-life detecting heroes are men and women who, as well as having an acute eye for discrepancies, also have wide experience of the hinterland of human nature. The

Yard's universal image is of a place that transcends class. Here the men and women are drawn from all sorts of backgrounds across the country, and their encyclopaedic knowledge of habitual criminals and the streets and districts in which they live, allows them to move largely unnoticed between the social strata. Whether it's an alley-haunting robbery look-out man or a languidly aristocratic murderer, Scotland Yard's detectives are expected to understand the common human motivations and criminal appetites that link them all.

We are also, of course, universally fascinated by the mind of the detective. Is the ability to make brilliant deductions a skill that can be taught? Or does one have to be born with the talent? Can eyes be trained to instantly take in all the details of a room in which a ghastly murder has taken place, and see the tiny clues – a drop of blood where it shouldn't be, a tiny scrap of paper beneath a glass – that elude everyone else?

The story of Scotland Yard has shown across the years that while alertness is definitely a talent that can be cultivated, a detective also needs what might seem like an odd combination of doggedness, slow patience, and sudden lightning-storm inspiration. The lightning is the glamorous part, but the doggedness is the most important. One of the constants in the story of Scotland Yard is the institution's devotion to facts, not only of names and places and past deeds, but also the history of pubs and clubs, businesses both legitimate and marginal. When pulled together, through referencing, cross-referencing and double checking, these facts become a library of the streets stored in the head of every great Yard detective.

Lastly, we must acknowledge that part of the enduring affection for and fascination with Scotland Yard derives from a universal appetite for challenging, enigmatic puzzles. This is certainly the case in fiction – each reader seeking to out-think Agatha Christie, and each reader always failing – but it is also the case in real life, too. What sort of a puzzler's mind must a detective have? The stereotyped aptitude for cryptic crosswords? The possibility-juggling challenge of Sudoku? Or the fact-sifting long-term analytical skills demanded by classical logic problems?

And what of that puzzler's psyche when faced with a criminal intent on setting out ever more devious challenges? Throughout the years there have been a variety of quite extraordinary jewellery and safe heists across London in which the question was not only who carried out the crime, but how was the crime carried out in the first place? Later in the book, we shall see such examples, including the diamonds that were apparently turned into lumps of coal, and the thief who apparently managed to be simultaneously in Kent and over 150 miles away in Somerset, seen by scores of honest witnesses.

The goal of a detective is clearly not only to solve the crime, but also to find the means to outwit, out-think and finally catch the perpetrator before a permanent escape can be made. In these terms, the detective is sometimes working against a time limit, a new twist of tension in an already difficult job.

We have all daydreamed, at one time or another, about whether we could become great detectives. Is there a fearsome written exam to be passed, filled with lateral logic problems and knotty questions about the law? Actually, there have been exams for decades and within these pages, among the other puzzles, you will find some vintage examples of the head-scratchers that were set for those who wished to be promoted to Detective Sergeant.

Further puzzles within these pages are designed to reflect a range of other skills required by all the very best detectives: quick-wittedness; the willingness to worry at a problem, gnawing at it until you reach the core of it; the ability to keep a step ahead of your opponents; and the priceless talent for taking a problem and turning it on its head to find a completely new approach towards the solution.

When faced with apparently impossible conundrums in the 1940s – tracking down a violent assailant using only a tiny scrap of cloth torn from the attacker's pocket, or pursuing an elegant cat-burglar who committed his crimes in full evening dress, leaving no prints or marks behind – Robert Fabian, one of Scotland Yard's finest detectives, used to say to himself: 'Give your eyes a chance.' That is, size up the problem, look not only at it, but around it too. As we will see, while Scotland Yard has always developed exciting new detection innovations and works of scientific wonder, none of these would be effective without detectives simply using their eyes and wits. Here then are over a hundred puzzles that aim to put you in the detectives' shoes and ask: have you got what it takes?

CHAPTER ONE

WHAT HAVE WE HERE?

There is a pitch-black irony in the fact that Scotland Yard itself once became the centre of a macabre murder mystery.

It began when the headquarters were being rebuilt in autumn 1888. As workmen hauled white Portland stone and thousands of red bricks into place to bring architect Norman Shaw's vision into being, an excavation of an old vault on the site yielded a hideous discovery: the body of a dismembered woman wrapped in black cloth, tied up with string. The newspapers were jumping up and down with excitement. Here, on this site between the banks of the Thames and Downing Street itself, was the sort of murder that Scotland Yard's detectives were now internationally famed for tackling.

All the newest techniques of the Yard were brought to bear upon this perplexing puzzle in its own precincts. The body had lain in the darkness of that cellar for a relatively short time, and police surgeon Thomas Bond was able to match it to an arm that had been found a short distance away on the Thames foreshore. He was also able to determine that the victim had been a woman about 24 years old and that she had been wearing a satin dress at the time of the murderous attack.

The national scope of Scotland Yard kicked in and detectives were able to pinpoint the fact that the dress had been made in Bradford, and the dress's pattern had last been used by that firm some three years previously. Surgeons and detectives were able to establish that the victim had not been in any trade that required hard physical labour. Tragically, though, it proved impossible to pinpoint the cause of death and the mystery remains unsolved to this day. But the Norman Shaw Scotland Yard buildings – the red brick alternating with the white stone in horizontal layers – were finished regardless and quickly became a national landmark and centre for ground-breaking criminology. The puzzles in this chapter reflect those early days of policing: tricky mental work-outs and tangential brainteasers, and an induction into sharp-eyed quick-wittedness.

The Metropolitan Police was established in 1829 after the Home Secretary Sir Robert Peel decided that law enforcement for the dark, grimy streets of the fast-growing capital should be centralised and not left to local parishes. From the start the Met was based close to Downing Street, at Scotland Yard. Sir Robert's inspiration saw an initial staff of 895 constables, 88 sergeants, 20 inspectors and 8 superintendents. By 1888, the institution was world-renowned and those new headquarters, mystery corpse aside, reflected the character of this proud body. The corridors within were said to be rambling and labyrinthine, but in a way, this was appropriate for an institution that specialised in detecting and exploring the mazes of the criminal mind.

Part of the enduring fascination of Scotland Yard involves the steps that one must take in order to become a detective. This is a line of work like no other. There is the sense of being inducted into secrets; an idea of arcane, esoteric knowledge. From the very start of the first detective department in 1842, some thirteen years after the Metropolitan Police was founded, the public have been mesmerised by the investigator's blend of preternatural perspicacity blended with low-down street cunning.

One of the most dramatic initial cases to be confronted by detectives at the Yard was known as The Bermondsey Horror. Marie La Roux was a Swiss national who had moved to London and was working as a maidservant for the grand society hostess Lady Blantyre. She was stepping out with – and later married – a man very far from that gilded milieu. Frederick Manning had a murky past and a track record of thieving. After their marriage the couple plotted and the cunning Marie found herself a rich lover, an administrator at the London docks called Patrick O'Connor, who had become disproportionately wealthy by making loans and charging high interest.

Marie invited her lover for dinner at her marital home in the south London suburb of Bermondsey, and at some point in the evening, O'Connor was murdered. The couple buried his body under the flagstones of the kitchen and Marie swiftly took herself to O'Connor's smart lodgings in Mile End and helped herself to certificates detailing his extensive share portfolios. Double-crossing her husband Frederick, she then escaped into the night with the lion's share of the bounty. With what ill-gotten loot was left, Frederick also fled. Marie booked herself a ticket on one of the new steam locomotives that now ran all the way to Scotland, while Frederick's train journey took him to Southampton, from whence he set sail to Jersey.

Both Marie and Frederick might have been confident that they could get away with it, but the absence of Patrick O'Connor – and gossip from his landlady about the loose morals of Marie Manning – led detectives and constables to the house in Bermondsey. They examined the abandoned property with care and came at last to the kitchen. After diligently poking around with trowels, they partially lifted a flagstone, and discovered the remains.

Here began an early high-speed manhunt with the police finding novel technological means of tracking down their quarry. Superintendent Haynes, following a tip from the driver of a horse-drawn cab, made enquiries at the grand terminus of Euston and was able to establish through witnesses that a well-dressed woman with a heavy French accent had the previous day bought a ticket to the Scottish capital. Haynes then utilised the Met's new technological marvel, the telegraph, to communicate instantly with Edinburgh colleagues. She had arrived in the city and had found lodgings. Indeed, Haynes learned that the Scottish police were investigating Marie for another reason: they had been tipped off that a lady with a French accent was attempting to sell suspiciously large quantities of railway stock. And so it was that the Scottish police moved in, and Marie was returned to London by rail, under police escort. Swifter travel also figured in the arrest of her husband; with Detective Langley speedily travelling by rail to the south coast, and thence sailing by steam to the Isle of Jersey, where he followed a trail of drunken boorish behaviour in hotels that led to Frederick Manning's side.

The husband and wife killers were executed together; a rare and unusually macabre event that earned the disapproval of none other than Charles Dickens.

But from the point of view of the police, the case had been a fine testing ground for a new age of velocity. By combining diligent detail – questioning everyone from landladies to cab drivers – and shrewd reasoning – where would the fugitives flee to? – the detectives set down the broad foundations for a new, wider-reaching way of policing. The public now began to see that the Yard had powers that could never have been imagined in decades previously; a national reach that made it difficult for criminals to evade their attention; and a knack for analysing the criminal mind, enabling them eventually to catch up with their prey.

And nor was this skill merely confined to horrible murder: it extended to thefts and frauds and other transgressions. Indeed, in response to the Yard's growing cerebral muscle, some criminals themselves became more sophisticated; jewel robberies, for instance, were planned with the meticulous care of an architect or landscape artist.

In the mid-nineteenth century, there was a case involving a luxurious London hotel and a spate of baffling thefts from within its rooms. The hotel management knew that the crimes could not possibly have been committed by someone wandering in off the street, nor indeed breaking in around the back. Their security was simply too fine for that. The detective assigned to the case approached the mystery with guile; rather than focusing on the items that had been stolen he decided to look at what had NOT been taken from the rooms that had been broken into. In one such room, he found a gentleman's shirt with one button missing. And it is this clue that unlocked the mystery, for in another room he found a corresponding button. The solution was socially unthinkable, yet it was the only possible answer. The thief was one of the hotel's grand guests, who had somehow gained access to keys, and had lost the button throughout the course of his burglarising mission. The evidence was circumstantial but the guest quickly confessed.

This was a case with no fingerprints or DNA; just a moment of insight prompted by the most raptor-eyed observation. Sometimes cases of theft need a different sort of sensitivity, that of a spider feeling the tiniest vibrations along the threads of a huge and complex web. This breakthrough came not so much from a eureka moment as the ability to interpret those tiny stirrings of the thread.

Another such case was that of the serial thief Harry Williams, who pulled off audacious thefts in the late nineteenth century and came to be known to the Yard and to the criminal underworld as 'Harry the Valet'. The particular crime that had the newspapers levitating with excitement was the spiriting away of pearls and other stones set in gold which belonged to the Dowager Duchess of Sutherland and were almost beyond value. The story began with a perfect head-scratcher.

When the theft occurred in the summer of 1899, the Duchess was travelling from Paris to London – a first class journey by train and Channel steam boat – with her husband Sir Albert Rollitt MP plus a couple of domestic servants and a number of her relatives. In her portmanteau were pearls and jewellery valued then at £30,000, a figure that would run into the millions today. The fascination with the robbery lay in this: how did a thief, presumably from the lower orders, gain access to this guarded sanctum of wealth?

The answer to this was threefold. First, Harry the Valet – who was later to write highly romanticised accounts of his life of crime – didn't dress like a member of the lower orders. He blended in by dressing in the same style as his victims. Secondly, he had a talent, especially at railway stations, for looking sufficiently distracted and harassed to evade any second glances, while keeping a keen eye on his prey. His warped genius lay in spotting the exact moment of maximum distraction – in this case, a great number of platform farewells at the Gare du Nord amid swirling crowds, noise and smoke. Thirdly, he did his research. Prior to their journey across the Channel, Harry had staked out the Duchess and her staff, observing their habits and movements. He prepared himself carefully and swooped with split-second precision when the entire party was focused on boarding the train.

The detective assigned to the case was Frank Froest who had an unusual reputation among his colleagues – and indeed known criminals – for wild physical strength. It was said that he could tear a pack of playing cards in two. However what he needed for this case was a certain amount of mental stability first to deal with the pressure of the Duchess's incandescent fury but also, working on the assumption that the thief was British and had returned, to somehow track down this elusive, unspotted figure.

As clues to the nature and timing of the crime were few and far between, Froest decided to keep a close eye on the sorts of pawnbrokers and rather less scrupulous tradesmen through whom stolen jewels might be sold on, while staying alert to London gossip of unlikely figures suddenly flashing some cash.

'Harry the Valet' was one such man, having been observed spending freely around the pubs of South Kensington. He had always been a flashy dresser but his expenditure was causing even old acquaintances to raise eyebrows. Froest and his young colleague Walter Dew (who was later to help run Dr Crippen to ground, as we shall see in chapter 3) managed to track down a disaffected girlfriend; and from thence to an address on the Fulham Road where they lay in wait for their quarry. The detective had been alert to every vibration along that thread of the web; and now his quarry was stuck fast. Harry the Valet received seven years, though according to his own account, had the vengeful last laugh of refusing to disclose what had happened to a significant number of the jewels that he had stolen. Still, Froest had his man.

The cases outlined above are intended as an induction into deduction. A quick historical taste of how everyday detectives faced crimes that were quite out of the ordinary and set about them with common sense and organisation. Uniting them, no matter the apparent complexity of the problem or enigma, is a refusal to accept the possibility of insolubility. For this reason, the detective's mind must not only be open but also, fundamentally, optimistic too.

Nothing within the bounds of human nature is beyond the wit of man, or woman, to solve.

And so the puzzles in this section are themselves intended as a rough induction; fast, furious, twisty, and filled with points at which even the most dedicated puzzle enthusiast will throw the pencil aside with frustration. But that moment of frustration might just be the one immediately prior to the bright light of revelation. This refusal to give up intrinsically links the first Victorian detectives of the Met with the fantastically agile crime fighters of today.

1

ON THE FRONT LINE

Look at the words below. Make it to the front line by finding a word which can go in front of each set of words listed.

1	AXE	FIELD	SHIP
2	BAKED	MAST	TRUTH
3	BOAT	LINE	SENTENCE
4	CARD	HORN	MILL
5	CHANGE	LEGS	LION
6	CASE	MATCH	TUBE
7	DROP	GROUND	NUMBER
8	FALL	POUR	TRODDEN
9	FINGERS	GROCER	HOUSE
10	ORGAN	PIECE	WATERING

2

SAFE NUMBER

A bank manager has vanished and no one knows the full combination of the locked safe. Individual members of staff, however, can recall pieces of information.

* The safe number used the digits 1 to 7 and each appeared once.

* No two odd digits are next to each other.

* The difference between adjacent digits is always greater than one.

* The penultimate digit was twice the value of the final digit.

This information is enough for the Inspector to work out the code and open the safe.

What was the code number?

3

ON YOUR BIKE

A British bobby and a bicycle go together like a horse and cart or fish and chips. The question is, which bicycle appears in the most rectangles in the drawing?

4

HIDDEN GEMS

It's not just stealing the gems which presents a problem, it's where to hide them before you sell them on, or how to successfully send a ransom note to their owner without being caught. The names of precious gems are hidden in the sentences below. Find them by joining words or parts of words together.

1   He is going to chop a lot of logs for the fire.

2   I am leaving for my train trip early tomorrow morning.

3   The crook dressed as a beggar netted a good haul of valuable items.

4   Rest assured, I am on duty this evening and you are in safe hands.

5   Is that the shrub you only planted last year? It's beautiful!

6   Escape. Rid others of your presence here!

5

POST HASTE

Portable posts are used in setting up barricades to block off roads or crime scenes. These particular posts are hexagonal. They were hastily stacked in a storage cupboard and haven't made best use of the space. What's the most number of posts that could have been stacked in the cupboard?

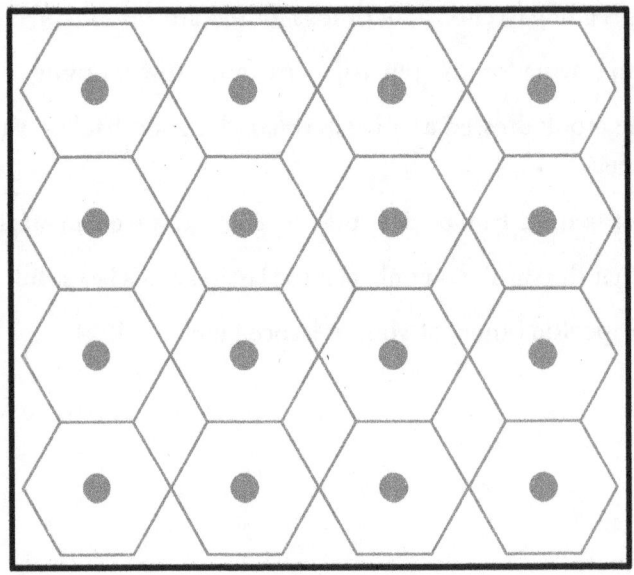

6

WEB OF INTRIGUE

Solve the clues below and slot the answers into the spider's web. Each answer starts in a numbered space, with remaining letters moving inwards to the centre of the web. The clues are in no particular order. When the answers are in place the two shaded areas read clockwise will spell out the name of a famous London location.

CONCLUDES

MELODY

EGG-SHAPED

BARRED OR WIRED PEN

REQUIRE

WORD INDICATING ACTION

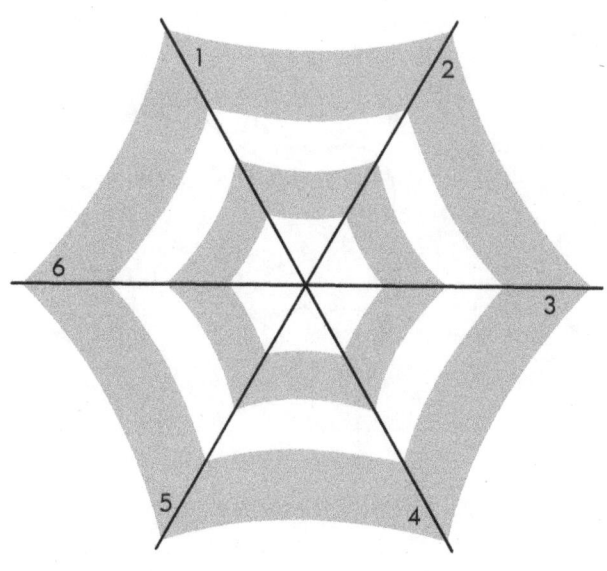

7

KEY QUESTION

The wealthy Victorians loved to fill their houses with fine furniture, books, ornaments and artwork. Having valuable possessions meant a greater need for security which in turn meant the mass production of locks, bolts and keys.

Here is a collection of keys. There are only two keys that are identical. This challenge requires a sharp eye. Which keys are the same?

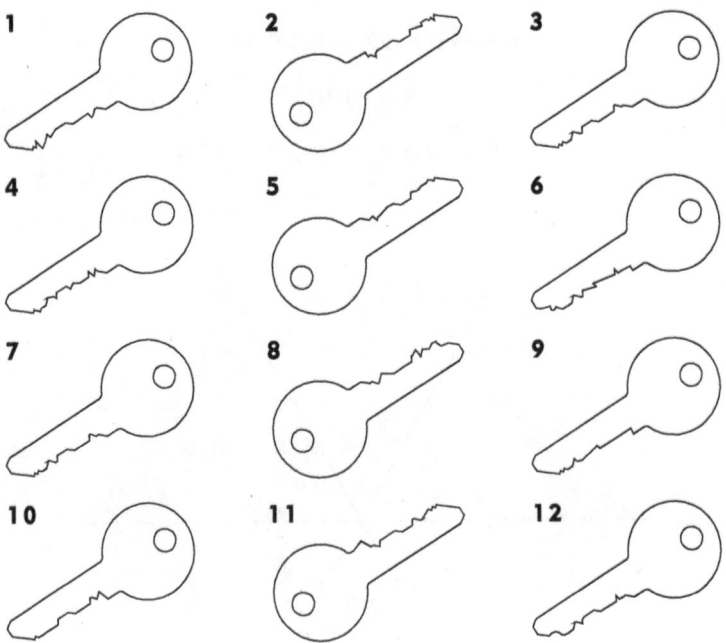

8

CHEERS!

There are six glasses in a row.
Three are empty.
Three are full.
You can only move or touch one glass.
Make a line in which all the glasses are alternately empty and full.

9

LINKS

Detective work often involves discovering a series of links and joining together clues that do not seem connected. Here's a note that was left behind at the scene of a crime.

Can you work out what the message conveys?

1 SKELETON (_ _ _) RING

2 RUG (_ _) GONE

3 IN (_ _ _ _) WAY

4 LOT (_ _) WARDS

5 ROB (_ _ _) SIDE

6 DARK (_ _ _ _) MATE

7 SOME (_ _ _) SELF

10

SHEER SKULDUGGERY

You are coming to the end of the first chapter of this book. The limbering up exercises are over and you have a taste for what lies ahead. It's now time to find the real detectives amongst you. The gloves are off and there is no fair play when it comes to crime!

Can you solve these brainteasers?

1   Hendon Police College opened in the 1930s. Which word was consistently spelt incorrectly on exam papers in its early days?

2   In the last century what could travel around the world and always stayed in the same corner?

3   An ill wind blows no one any good. Such was the case when a gust of wind blew off all the helmets belonging to ten police officers while they were on crowd control duty. Fortunately, a couple of nimble young lads came to the rescue, scooped them all up, and returned them to their rightful owners. What is the probability that nine police officers each received his own helmet?

4   You follow a suspect to a notorious East End hostelry. He nods to the barman and asks for a glass of H, I, J, K, L, M, N, O. What happened next?

5   Peter the pickpocket returned home with a banknote he had eased out of a gentleman's pocket. When asked where he got it from he said he had found it inside a book, someone must have been using it as a bookmark. When asked which pages he answered, 'between pages 5 and 6'. Was he believed?

CHAPTER TWO

HUE AND CRY

Truly great detectives have always had the wisdom to see that sometimes it takes the intertwining of intelligence, inspiration and good fortune to solve the most knottiest cases, and this was even more true before the advent of forensics. The early days of Scotland Yard now provide a fascinating insight into the inspirational deductions of long ago – the way that detecting minds worked on the trickiest of cases without the fallback of technology.

Accordingly, the puzzles in this section have a period flavour about them. A series of challenges calculated to produce chewed lower lips while suggesting something of historical criminals who deliberately set out not only to deceive, but also to bedazzle with apparent impossibilities. And here we go back even further in time than the formation of Scotland Yard, to the ancestors of the Met, the Bow Street Runners.

In the 1700s, the primitive policing for the city was carried out by watchmen and parish constables, and was simply not sufficient for the maze-like and teeming streets of London with their ever-widening range of crimes. Parish councils employed 'thief takers', an early form of arresting officer, whose job it was to catch felons and bring them before the magistrate. But the work was difficult and dangerous and gained no respect either from criminals or law-abiding members of the public.

The novelist Henry Fielding, best known today for his rambunctious *Tom Jones*, was to change this; he was also a magistrate. His house in Bow Street, near Covent Garden, doubled as an extemporised court, and in 1749 he and his brother, Sir John, had the idea of recruiting a group of men whose job it would be to apprehend suspects. These men – six of them at first – became known as the Bow Street Runners. They were initially funded by the Fielding brothers themselves, but after a few years this would change and they would be the first kind of police funded by the government. The Fieldings made it quite clear that for investigations to have any solid legitimacy, and indeed the respect of communities, the men carrying them out had to have the official backing of the state.

Sir John Fielding was blind but his insight was strong. At this time, many crimes went unsolved simply because criminals moved around the country and there was no centralised record system or way of keeping track of them. Magistrates in the north, when faced with wrong-doers who stood before them under assumed identities, claiming to be from towns in the south, had no means of checking, other than sending messages to grand local social acquaintances in the hope they might help.

And so it was that Sir John Fielding laid down the first foundation stone of a national crime database, a means not only of holding details of each offender, but also a way of alerting others in far away parts that an offender was in their midst. The hot new media of the late 1700s was the newspaper, and so Sir John produced a special version, intended for circulation among town crime fighters up and down the land. It was called *Hue and Cry*.

This newspaper publicised every crime committed: from forgery of papers to theft of antiques, from violent assault to the darkest murders. The reports carried all the relevant details of these murky cases and when there were suspects, they were named, alongside their full descriptions. By this method – combined with the then dazzlingly fast new services of the Royal Mail, which could carry letters across the country under an unprecedentedly efficient system at speeds of just a few days – criminal profiles began to be built. And with these profiles came the first glimmering of the discipline of criminology: the first sense that patterns could be detected in the actions of certain antisocial recidivists.

Thieves would have had their own idiosyncratic methods; and murderers too would have had a signature style, occasionally unmistakeable. This was the beginning, in effect, of the first criminal database and also the first time that it became clear there was a general fascination with the contest between criminals and law-enforcers. As well as publishing *Hue and Cry*, Sir John Fielding ensured that popular newspapers received regular briefings from his Bow Street office about the ghastliest and most extraordinary of crimes. Both he and subsequent generations of newspaper editors were to find that there was an enormous public appetite for reading of wrong-doings; and a concomitant appetite to read about those who would solve these mysteries.

The detective department of Scotland Yard – which in 1878 became the Criminal Investigation Department, reformed after a serious case of internal corruption – was founded in a world where the mind was understood in quite a different way from today. Sigmund Freud was yet to turn established notions of motive and impulse on their heads. Added to this, perfectly rational though Victorian detectives were, they were moving through a society that was susceptible in many ways to unexplained phenomena: the rise of spiritualism was the respectable face of the more common belief in ghosts. There are innumerable cases throughout the late 1800s of London suburbs such as Islington and villages near Manchester and Birmingham that succumbed to ghost hysteria: huge crowds gathering in churchyards at midnight in the belief that particular ghosts would walk the yew-lined paths. It was the detectives who had to unmask the spectral troublemakers who were hoping to whip up riotous anarchic behaviour.

Also, before the 1870s, there was next to nothing in the way of forensics (in one 1860 murder case, the most sophisticated item of evidence was a bloody boot-print on a floorboard that was patiently sawed around and presented to the court as though it answered any questions at all). These same detectives had to keep their heads when criminals apparently pulled off feats that were beyond the realm of physics. One such case came in the very earliest years of the department, and it involved a man who was in two different places at exactly the same time: the sort of feat that even today's quantum physicists would dismiss as science fiction.

The crime was a theft from a mail coach (just before the ever-expanding railway network handled all such business) riding through Kent towards London carrying a substantial sum of money. The actual purloining, it was understood, must have happened at a coaching inn not far from Canterbury.

The police had a shrewd idea of the culprit: a man who had been seen by some witnesses and also had form in this area. The only difficulty was that when he was apprehended, the man concerned told them quite calmly that they were wholly mistaken and he could prove it: he had been in Taunton at the time the robbery was carried out, and there were large numbers of independent witnesses who could corroborate his story. And, indeed, as the police found to their frustration, it was true. He had been in Taunton.

The trouble was that the police knew from even more reliable witnesses that he had also been at that coaching inn just outside Canterbury. He was the man in two places.

Obviously he could not be convicted – and so he went free – but the man in two places conundrum continued to perplex the officers. That is, until the day that he was seen up a ladder – when he was simultaneously working at another house further up the street. The one possibility that everyone had overlooked – the one, incidentally, never allowed by the majority of crime authors as it is just too implausible – was that the man in two places was in fact a twin.

One figure who revelled in such mysteries was Charles Frederick Field. He had been among the very first to join the Yard's detective branch in 1842, having spent a decade as a constable around London's most poverty-haunted districts; and indeed, Inspector Field was also the first detective to rise to public prominence and a certain measure of fame. Even though he was no longer on patrols, the Inspector continued to visit London's rookeries (this was the term for the poorest of dwellings, always over-crowded, dark, rotting, running with damp, smelling foul and incubators of both disease and crime) and on one night, he was joined on his urban rounds by the author Charles Dickens, who was fascinated beyond measure by Field's detective work, and wished to write about it for his popular journal

Household Words. The detective and the author made their way from obscenely broken-down lodging houses in St Giles to a den of habitual offenders in Borough – then back over the river to Whitechapel to inspect the premises of a local villain known for employing thieves.

But Inspector Field had other responsibilities too, at the more fragrant end of society, and he could often be found making his rounds in the eerie night-time galleries of the British Museum, ensuring that no-one was making off with treasure or, indeed, with Egyptian mummies. Another of his assignments involved Lord Lytton, who had written a play – *Not So Bad As We Seem* – which was to open in a theatre near the Strand. The detective was sent to act as Lord Lytton's bodyguard because Lytton had received some sinister anonymous threats.

Inspector Field – who might at first have been expecting some kind of assassination attempt – dug a little further into where these threats might have been coming from and soon deduced that they were chiefly the work of his lordship's estranged wife Rosina. It seemed that the threat was not quite as dangerous as expected and consisted largely of Rosina disguising herself as an orange seller and then, during the performance, unleashing a volley of rotten fruit upon the stage. That particular assault, although thwarted, was perhaps understandable in the light of his Lordship's previous dreadful behaviour toward Rosina. Indeed, a few years after that he had her incarcerated in an asylum for a month; an outrage that partly inspired Wilkie Collins's *The Woman In White.*

Incidentally, if that particular case seemed somehow a little light for the detective branch, it is worth bearing in mind that a few decades later, a lot of Sherlock Holmes's cases involved juicy society scandals wrapped up in mysteries rather than always being a hunt for a killer.

Moving fluidly between social strata, early detectives of both the Bow Street runners and the CID had to cultivate a vital sense of detachment from social judgements; their job was simply to unravel brain-boggling mysteries, and to identify and catch those who were guilty of crimes. They were the dispassionate agents of truth. The puzzles in this section reflect a need for emotionless analysis: the more baroque the mystery (just as in the real life case of the body-snatchers Burke and Hare, who went from digging up bodies for medical researchers, to simply murdering people to keep the level of supply up), the cooler the eye has to be. There is nothing to be gained from rushing to solutions; here are vintage mysteries instead that have to be teased out, even if it becomes a waiting game. The most modern detectives, with access to an entire world's worth of databases updated in real time, abide by the same principles as their eighteenth-century forerunners. Let's see if you can make them work for you, too.

1

THE BODY SNATCHERS

The notorious Burke and Hare were arguably the most famous body snatchers of all time, moving from providing corpses for medical research to murder most foul. In the puzzle below complete the word by inserting the name of a body part, an exercise which demands looking with a cool eye, and keeping your mind open.

1 S _ _ _ M E N T

2 M A _ _ _ _ I S T

3 C _ _ _ B A G E

4 E C _ _ _ S E

5 W _ _ _ _ W R I G H T

6 E N _ _ _ _ _ _

7 P O T A _ _ _ S

8 I L _ _ _ I B L E

2

A BONE TO PICK

A gruesome task to carry out! This pile of bones needs to be examined and catalogued. In which order must you remove the bones so that you are always taking the top one off the pile?

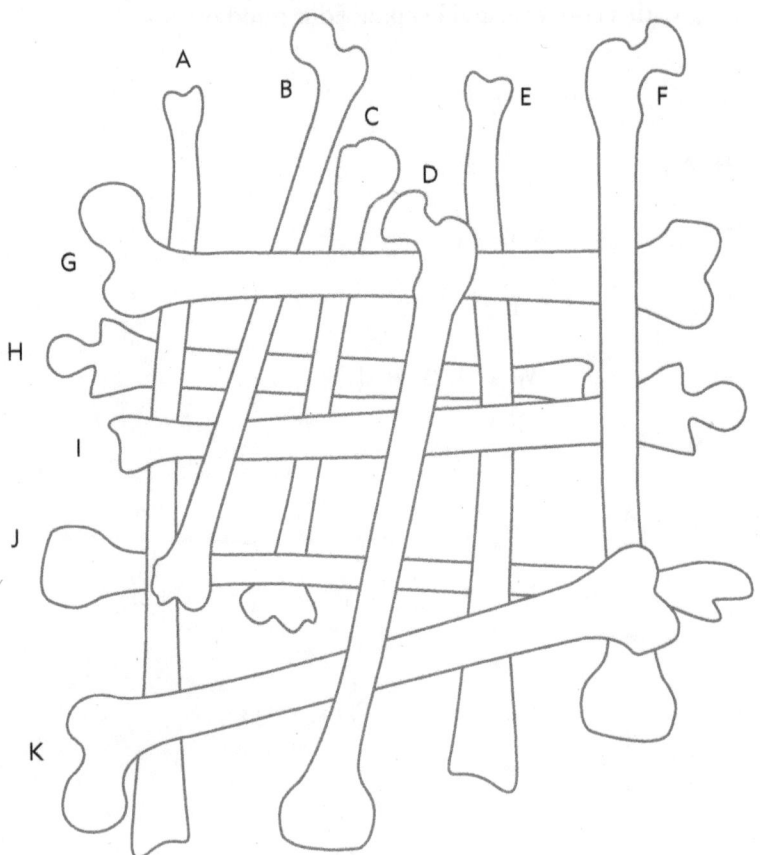

3

HUE AND CRY

No loud clamour here, just a call to complete this mix and match puzzle. Look at the list below and pair up the words. All words can be joined by 'and'. One word will be left over. What is it?

ADAM	ALBERT	ALL	ANTONY
BOLTS	BURKE	CAMBRIDGE	CLEOPATRA
CRIME	DAVID	DOMBEY	EVE
GILBERT	GOLIATH	HARE	HOLMES
HYDE	INK	JACK	JEKYLL
JILL	JULIET	LAW	LEARN
LIVE	NUTS	ORDER	OXFORD
PEN	PONY	PUNISHMENT	REMUS
ROMEO	ROMULUS	SON	SULLIVAN
TIME	TRAP	VICTORIA	WARTS
WATSON			

4

ALL CLUED UP

The early Victorian detectives were most frustrated with their cases just before they were solved. Here, you are in the same position! The Across clues are numbered as in a traditional crossword. The Down clues are in no particular order and are not numbered. All that you have to go on is the number of letters in the words. Trial and error, educated guesswork and determined doggedness will be needed to complete the puzzle with all the words in their correct place!

ACROSS

1   Strategies, moves (7)
5   Algebra, arithmetic, etc. (5)
8   Alternative identity (5)
9   Method, procedure (7)
10 Not a single person (6)
12 Noted down (6)
13 Keen, enthusiastic (5)
14 Sombre, unlit (4)
15 Semi precious stone (4)
17 Robber (5)
19 Looked for (6)
21 Passenger ships (6)
24 Person under surveillance (7)
25 Play (5)
26 Outmoded (5)
27 Here (7)

DOWN

Not outside (6)
Length of cotton or wool (6)
Make ready (7)
Put your faith in (5)
Sailing boat (5)
Put an end to (4)
Mountaineer (7)
No longer in service (7)
Locomotive and carriages (5)
Secure (4)
Gem (5)
Shame, dishonour (7)
Cook the books! (6)
Reflect (6)
Clever, astute (5)
In some distress (5)

5

VOWEL PLAY

Not just suspected . . . vowel play has definitely occurred here! Names of some of the shadier parts of Victorian London have had their consonants stolen. Only the vowels have been left behind. Can you right the wrong?

1 _ _ I _ E _ _ A _ E _

2 _ I _ E / E _ _

3 _ O _ _ I _ _ / _ I _ _

4 _ A _ _ _ E _

5 _ E _ _ _ A _ / _ _ E E _

6 _ O _

6

SHADY CHARACTER

Look at the words below. Rearrange the letters in each word to create a new word and put that word reading Across in the blank grid. When this is complete, one column reading Down will give you the name of an eminent Victorian who had deep rooted concerns about the poor in Victorian society, and how this linked to the criminal world. Now take the letters in the shaded squares to spell out the name of one of the shadiest characters in Victorian literature.

1						
S	E	C	U	R	E	S

2						
F	R	E	I	G	H	T

3						
B	A	S	T	I	O	N

4						
C	A	V	I	A	R	E

5						
C	I	T	A	D	E	L

6						
E	N	L	A	R	G	E

7						
S	I	M	I	L	E	S

8						
D	A	N	G	L	E	D

9						
B	R	I	G	A	D	E

10						
C	O	R	P	S	E	S

11						
I	R	K	S	O	M	E

12						
D	E	C	R	E	E	D

13						
E	L	A	T	I	O	N

14						
F	L	E	M	I	S	H

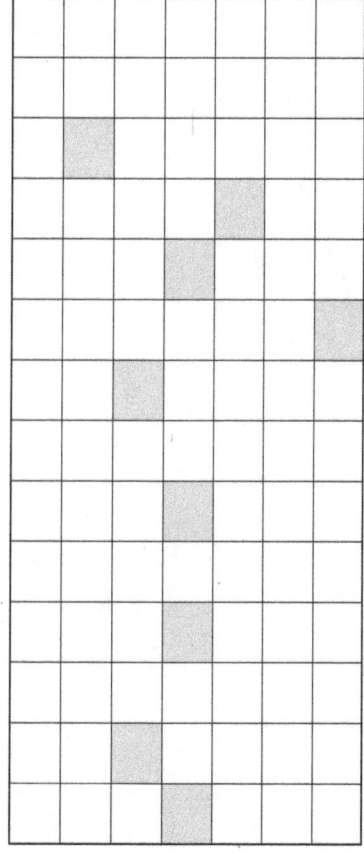

7

IN-FILL-TRATE

Infiltrating criminal gangs to gain information is a vital, but highly dangerous task.

Find a three-letter word, which fills the gaps and creates new words in each group. The words taken in order form a saying that was very apt for the early police force and for Scotland Yard.

1 G _ _ _ O N
    W _ _ _ E T
    S Q U _ _ _ Y

5 S W O _ _ _ _ D
    L I _ _ _ S S
    B A R _ _ _ T

2 _ _ _ K
    C O M _ _ _ T
    E N _ _ _ C E

6 A F _ _ _ D
    _ _ _ G E
    U N I _ _ _ M

3 D R _ _ _ D
    H _ _ _ S T Y
    P I _ _ _ E R

7 V _ _ _ E Y
    S C _ _ _ O P
    U S U _ _ _ Y

4 C _ _ _ L E
    M E _ _ _ E R
    V E R _ _ _ A

8

THE MURDER MUSEUM

The Murder Museum houses the most gruesome exhibits connected to most foul of crimes. However, there are worse things afoot, as the Chief Curator of the Murder Museum has been found dead in one of the rooms. The suspects are all employees of the Museum and each have a particular room that they are responsible for. The Curator's final act was to fall forward and leave these blood-stained finger prints on the wall.

Is it chance that has led him to leave blood-stains on this particular picture on the wall, amidst a display of hieroglyphics? Is there a clue here that could lead to his assailant?

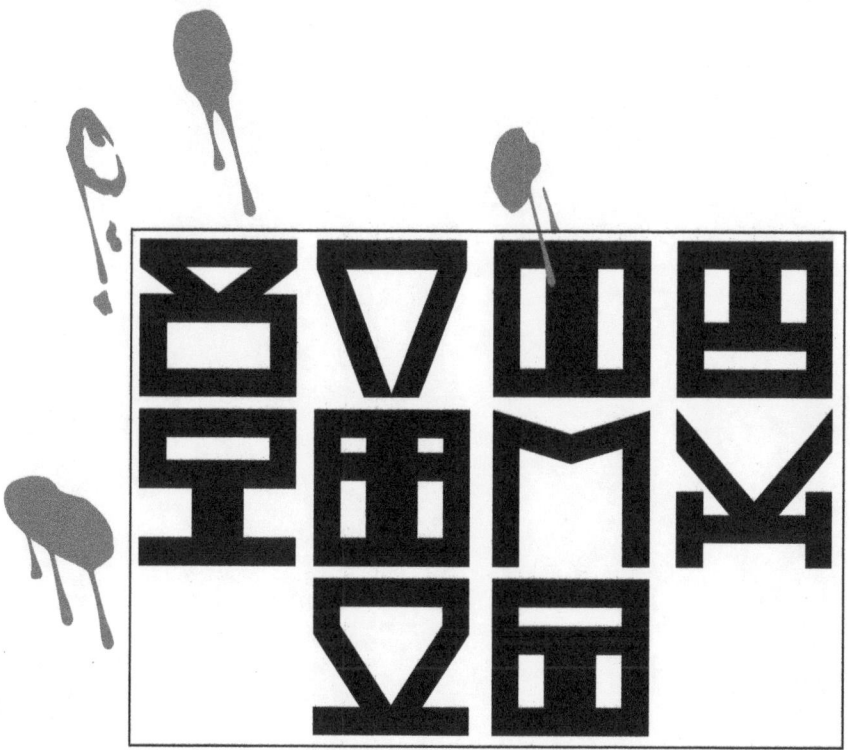

CHAPTER THREE

THE TEST TUBE TRIUMPHS

If you make any kind of contact, you will leave a trace. In a high-tech world, even so much as a molecule left behind will be enough to confirm your presence. It's easy to assume that crime-scene analysis is a very modern area of detective work, but the principle was actually formulated in 1904, by a scientist called Edmond Locard. 'Every constant leaves a trace,' he said, thus inaugurating the discipline of forensics. From mud on shoes to fibres on chairs, any evidence drawn from the crime scene, anything that the transgressor touched, would bear some trace of his person. It was almost as though Locard could see the microscopic DNA-dominated future. In any case, detectives, whose job it is not merely to envisage and imagine crime scenes, but also to deduce the identity of the participants of those scenes, have always been keenly interested in the physical tokens that can help point to guilt.

For instance, a fingerprint found in 1902 in a billiard room in a smart house in hilly suburban London helped secure the conviction of a serial burglar using magnifying glasses and up-to-the-minute photography. This was the very first time that such prints were used as evidence in the Old Bailey. The thief had made off with all the billiard balls; but had left a particularly clear set of fingerprints on the window-sill.

Slightly stranger was the 1950s case of the bare footprint on top of a television set, which led to a surprise conviction. The scene of the crime: the fourth floor flat of Mrs Bowles. Before retiring to bed,

Mrs Bowles had left her newly washed underwear out to dry on the mantelpiece. Since her flat was sixty feet up, and presumed burglar-proof, she had left the window slightly open. But this serial burglar was a skilled climber and it was the underwear that he chose to take. Even more bizarrely, he committed the crime in bare feet. This was the first time such a print had been used in court.

These cases on their own might not sound like triumphs of technical wizardry, but the fact is that under either the hiss of gaslight or the pitiless glare of modern LED spotlights, Scotland Yard has always been consistent in its enthusiasm for scientific innovation.

In fact, nowadays, a crime scene is a laboratory. Everything must be handled with care so that the conditions remain in a state of perfect equilibrium. And this laboratory – the scene of a daring heist or a shocking attack – is one in which the tiniest molecules serve to build a picture of human passion and intrigue. Clues are pieced together from a single strand of hair, an atom of paint from a location far off, or a fragment of clothing.

The puzzles in this section are inspired by the breathtaking leaps in scientific understanding that have been made by the experts at Scotland Yard. From the simplest magnifying glasses to the very structure of DNA, these puzzles celebrate the dazzling armoury of technological advancement that detectives have been able to deploy. These new inventions do not reduce or replace the detective's innate brilliance at weighing and understanding the souls of suspects, rather they complement such understanding.

A fascination with the idea of guilt being imputed by invisible tell-tale signs stretches right back through the centuries. From thirteenth-century China, a book entitled *The Washing Away Of Wrongs* made its way to the West along the Silk Road trade route through central Asia and, once translated, its ideas were instantly influential. From the careful examination of bodies and wounds, to methods for narrowing down rural suspects by testing whose sickle attracted the most flies, and therefore carried traces of blood, this was a text that stressed impartiality and an open mind when approaching suspected homicide. In the fourteenth century, the European rediscovery of this text led to autopsies being carried out in Bologna. This was the first effort made by dispassionate observers in the western world to locate and prove the cause of death. At a time when investigations of dead bodies carried a sharp frisson of religious sensitivity and danger, these autopsies were radical acts, but fascination with the disposition of the dead continued.

In a similar vein, the minute examination of everything from hair to teeth commenced with the arrival of the microscope in 1590. Its invention is broadly credited to father and son Hans and Zacharias Janssen. Owing to the astounding cost and expertise involved with working with glass, it was a long time before the study of optics could spread wide enough to have any impact when it came to crime. Yet the idea alone was sufficient to open minds to the world beyond the naked eye.

The greatest jump forward came in the 1670s from Antonie Van Leeuwenhoek with his self-designed single-lensed microscopes. This Dutchman took intense delight in subjecting samples from his own body to scrutiny, from fragments of tooth plaque to even less palatable items. This sparked a nineteenth-century hobbyist craze of seeing the weirdly animated world of any sort of fluid sample; something Leeuwenhoek termed 'animalcules'. Leeuwenhoek – who came to be honoured by the Royal Society in London – had opened up an entire realm in miniature: from bacteria to muscle fibres to spermatozoa. By doing so, he helped to revolutionise the way that the human body and each of its own individual signifiers, from red blood cells to capillaries, were seen. Every body could now be understood in terms of its own microscopic uniqueness.

Meanwhile, the study of fingerprints – which has somehow come to symbolise the entire business of detection – was adopted surprisingly slowly by Scotland Yard. By the 1860s, William Herschel, working with government officials in India, had come to see the individual properties of every single fingerprint. In a few cases, this led to them being used as legal identifying marks on documents requiring such proof. But for the detectives, there were two obstacles: first, the conclusive proof that fingerprints really were wholly unique, and second, the means by which to obtain them. Not every crime would handily feature prints left on a clear glass tumbler!

There was some competition in finding a way to uniquely identify suspects. In 1880s France, an anthropologist called Alphonse Bertillon constructed a new system that involved taking all the body measurements of offenders and suspects; the idea being that all of these elements together would create a unique profile. Meanwhile in Britain, the slightly less labour-intensive method of collecting fingerprints was given a boost by another anthropologist. Sir Francis Galton, a relation of Charles Darwin, wrote with a fresh authority about the absolute individuality of fingerprints, and by 1901, Scotland Yard was confident enough in the evidence to begin a proper classified register of fingerprints from convicted offenders.

Chemistry is another key element in the science of forensics, and it found its own uses as early as 1836. This was just on the cusp of what might frivolously be described as the golden age of Victorian poisoning: a period when the most remarkable proportion of murders seemed to involve the procurement of something lethal from the apothecary. It was James Marsh who formulated the first ever test for arsenic poisoning. In the years that followed, a cornucopia of new tests were devised for an ever-widening range of lethal elixirs.

Inspired by this poisonous period of history, Agatha Christie, the world's best-selling crime novelist, made close studies of poisons, their effects and the means by which they may be detected. Hence the unusually high instance of this form of murder in her novels.

Chemistry tests to determine between animal and human blood took a little longer to become in any way reliable. This proved a source of frustration in some late-nineteenth century cases where splashes of blood – presumed to be that of the victim – could not convincingly be used as evidence. Perhaps even more maddeningly for Scotland Yard, the author Arthur Conan Doyle gave his newly created detective a wildly unfair advantage; Sherlock Holmes had conveniently devised such a blood test in his fictional world. But perhaps Holmes was an inspirational spur. By 1900, the matter had been remedied, and indeed by that time different blood groups were identifiable too.

Holmes may also have been highly influential in other forensic matters, such as his method of identifying mud on a protagonist's shoe that could pinpoint precisely where in the country the shoe had been. The Yard did not care to cite Holmesian tricks as their inspiration, but French forensic genius Edmond Locard, and professors such as Charles Tidy who habitually helped the Yard, were happy to do so. They devoured the adventures of The Great Detective.

Edmond Locard, for his own part, was fascinated by the crime-solving properties of dust. He recognised that dust had a number of origins and if correctly analysed, could reveal some extraordinary surprises about who had been where. The principle of it, avowed another forensic pioneer, Dr Hans Gross, was quite simple. 'The dust of a ballroom,' he said (by means of example), 'crowded with people, will in great measure proceed from the fibres from which the cloth of the dancers is woven.'

Locard – and his Scotland Yard admirers – took the principle a little further. He was gripped by the variety of these 'mute witnesses', the 'microscopic debris' that testified, 'sure and faithful' to 'all our movements and encounters.' To him, there was something poetic in all the different sorts of dust, even down to the dust of dead butterflies, which fascinated him.

With these advances in detection, the men and women of the Yard were able to peer into the darkness of another realm, and experts, such as Professor Charles Tidy, were able to take them even further. In studying prone bodies of murder victims, lying where they fell, Professor Tidy could suggest what had happened, when, and at what angle. He could replay the sequence of events through looking at the shapes of the body's muscles pressed against the floor and the positions of tiny objects all around it. Each small detail gave away a part of the story.

A further tool – with distinctly macabre overtones – was given a terrible global fame by Scotland Yard in the autumn of 1888. What marked the hideous Jack the Ripper murders out was not just their terrifying savagery but also the imagery of those foggy Whitechapel streets that remains so prevalent today. But it was a new police tool that gave the case a further gruesome immortality: the pioneering use of photography. The victims, unknown in their poverty, acquired grisly posthumous celebrity with the portraits the Yard took of their mortuary table faces. Just a decade or so later, the French had perfected the techniques of photographing crime scenes. These dreadful black and white tableaux of slain bodies in hallways and boudoirs were so shocking they were later displayed in upmarket galleries and at prestigious exhibitions as fully fledged works of art.

On a practical level, the emotionless gaze of the lens was able to freeze in time all the tiny particulars that, in real life, were acquiring dust and contamination minute-by-minute.

Perhaps the figure who made the most lasting contribution to this new science of analysing crime scenes was a forensic pathologist who was to become a household name. Sir Bernard Spilsbury – who as we shall see was instrumental in solving some of the more lurid cases in the Yard's history – worked with detectives in formulating what were jocularly referred to as 'murder bags' but known properly as 'detective boxes'.

This was standardised equipment that detectives would use when approaching the scene of a horrible murder: a leather bag containing rubber (later plastic) gloves, tweezers (for handling minute objects), brushes, tape measures and evidence bags (for careful preservation of objects). This equipment became essential after Sir Bernard Spilsbury had seen policemen at crime scenes picking up all sorts of evidence with their bare hands; it would not do.

The principle of the murder bag remains the same today, even if the means of analysing the evidence collected is super-advanced. Sir Bernard Spilsbury laid the foundation stones of conserving evidence, alongside his developments in tissue analysis and other tests. He was the pathologist called to a darkened house on Hilldrop Crescent in 1910, in the sooty north London suburb of Holloway where deep in the cellar were found buried human remains; meanwhile, the house's occupant, one Dr Hawley Crippen, had made for the docks with his lover, and was on board a ship to America.

Sir Bernard, according to some accounts, was able to identify the grisly cellar discovery as Dr Crippen's wife by means of a tiny distinguishing mark on a small patch of skin.

The capture of Dr Crippen was – incidentally – a technological coup for Scotland Yard at the time. He was on board a ship called the *Montrose* with his lover disguised as a boy. It is perhaps little wonder that they were recognised by the captain. Thanks to advances in telegraphy between ships and back to London, plans were formulated to arrest Crippen before he could make land in the US, which was beyond the reach of British justice.

The ship's route took it through Canadian waters, making a number of stops on its way to the US. At the same time, the Yard's Inspector Dew was on board a steamship, sailing at full pelt across the Atlantic in pursuit. After another frantic flurry of shipboard telegrams, Dr Crippen's boat drew close to Quebec along the Lawrence river, and the ship was met with a team of pilots. Among them, in disguise, was Inspector Dew. And now, in the waters of a British dominion, he had his man. 'Good morning, Dr Crippen, do you know me?' he said. 'I'm Chief Inspector Dew from Scotland Yard.'

Sir Bernard Spilsbury was also key to the unravelling of the creepy 'Brides in the Bath' crimes. The mystery began in 1915, when a boarding house owner in the north was reading the *News of the World* and was struck by a story about a wife in Highgate, north London, who was found drowned in her bathtub. The husband had collected on the insurance. This boarding house owner was amazed because exactly the same tragedy had unfolded in his house two years previously. The husband had a different name; but he sent the newspaper clippings to Scotland Yard, convinced of a connection.

Detective Inspector Neil, intrigued, visited the house in Highgate and discovered that the bathtub in question was rather small, and that the deceased wife was rather portly. Here was a mystery: even if she had had a seizure or epileptic fit, how then could her head have become completely submerged? There was no room for natural manoeuvre. Meanwhile, a detective in Kent got in contact to say that there had been a near-identical incident in Herne Bay; a wife found drowned in her bath, and a cashed-in insurance policy.

The husbands in question were called Henry Williams, John Lloyd and George Smith. But they were in fact all the same man: a serial bigamist (George Smith was his real name) and as it seemed, a serial murderer too. It was down to the pathologist Sir Bernard Spilsbury to work out how all the wives were drowned, especially in the instance where the bathtub was so small. In a striking piece of active detective work, with Sir Bernard's advice, Inspector Neil hired several women volunteers who were experienced at diving. They donned their bathing suits and were invited to clamber into a specially-provided Scotland Yard tub. Inspector Neil tried pushing them under the water but the struggles and the noise – and indeed the failure to keep the women submerged – ruled that approach out. Spilsbury advised an alternative method, so Neil grabbed the ankles of one volunteer and pulled her head swiftly under the water; she lost consciousness almost instantly.

Sir Bernard's theory that a cranial nerve, when subjected to sudden submersion nasally and orally, could cause the victim to faint and thus to drown, was correct. The diver was revived, George Smith was convicted and the case was closed.

Sir Bernard approached other cases with distinct Holmesian flavourings: a solicitor who murdered a rival with a box of chocolates (the soft centres carefully injected with arsenic); and a Leighton Buzzard murderer identified by means of soil analysis, where the specks of mud in his trouser turn-ups matched the soil of a certain field where the crime took place.

From all of this, detectives became the archaeologists of crime. They knew that something as small as a burnt matchstick in an ashtray could open up entirely new avenues of exploration. Long before the crime scene became a modern circus of white tents populated by professional operatives in baggy white suits, Scotland Yard's finest were treating the scenes of murder like temples, in which nothing may be disturbed, and in which the past could be summoned and the guilty revealed.

And for detectives everywhere working on the molecular level, this is not merely about finding key details, but also about an entirely different way of looking at the world. Nothing can be taken at face value; everything, including the finest dust, must be interrogated for its true significance. Given the formidable armoury of scientific wizardry available now, one could be lured into mistakenly thinking that the art of detection can be handed over to computers. For surely a sample of soil and a single drop of blood, processed by artificial intelligence, would instantly find the culprit in a population of sixty-six million? In addition to this, all the software that can now not only recognise faces, but also individual gaits (the way we walk is almost as unique a signifier as fingerprints) must surely mean that no villain could ever escape justice?

Yet the world is much stranger and much more unpredictable than that. Even armed with DNA sequences drawn from crime scenes detectives must still ponder the mysteries of motivation, and the secret passions – hatred, envy or unrequited love – of the human heart.

1

A TO Z OF CRIME

26 clues, 26 answers each one beginning with a different letter of the alphabet. We give you the first letter and the length of the word. It is then up to you to fit the words back into the grid. Only the best detectives will crack this. There is only one solution.

A   Assisted an offender (7)

B   A policeman (5)

C   Telephone kiosk (4,3)

D   Word used to describe a suspicious character (7)

E   Escaped from capture (6)

F   Spokesman of the jury (7)

G   Procuring – by fair means or foul! (7)

H   Murders (9)

I   Seizes or ambushes goods or messages (10)

J   Precious gems (9)

K   A finger guard or a ring with a large stone (7,3)

L   Arresting phrase _____ be 'aving you! (4)

M   Bad luck (10)

N   Subtlety of meaning, so care needed to get it right (6)

O   Resist or thwart (6)

P   Authorisation given to a deputy (5)

Q   Enquiry (5)

R   Acquisition – of stolen goods maybe (7)

S   Secret sets of bones in a cupboard? (9)

T   Persistent; quality vital to get to the root of a problem (9)

U   Official police clothing (7)

V   Macabre watchers or spectators (7)

W   Targets for pickpockets (7)

X   Photographed through something opaque (1,5)

Y   A prison sentence might last a number of these (5)

Z   Enthusiasm (4)

2

ON THE LEVEL

Here's a picture of some apparatus from a laboratory. Two things cannot be right. What are they?

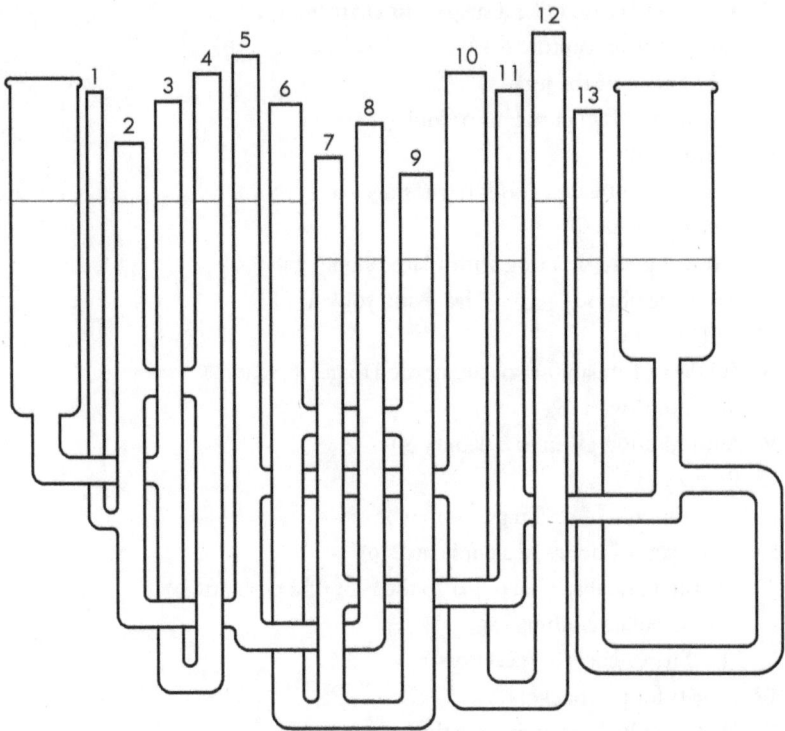

3

MEMORABLE MESSAGE

In this puzzle, your task is to uncover part of a famous message sent to Scotland Yard in the early part of the twentieth century. This message had a particular historic significance. Solve the straightforward clues below and write the answers in the upper grid. When this is complete take the letters in the shaded squares (four from answer 1 and three from the other answers) and slot them vertically in the lower grid. This will reveal the message.

1 Train stop
2 Saved from danger
3 Continent reached by crossing the Atlantic
4 Conquer a territory by force
5 Six sided shape
6 Large weapon used by an archer
7 Flying a plane without an engine
8 Red pepper
9 Seek votes and support from electors
10 Scottish city

4

HOURGLASS

Here are two hourglasses which contain sand. When the area full of sand is turned to be at the top it will start to filter down to the lower section. It's a device that dates back centuries and one that is remarkably accurate at keeping time.

One timer takes exactly NINE minutes for the sand to move from the top to the lower section. The other timer takes exactly FIVE minutes for the same thing to happen.

Your task is to find a way to measure THIRTEEN minutes using the two timers.

NINE MINUTES

FIVE MINUTES

5

ELEMENTARY

The periodic table was first developed in the nineteenth century. Use the symbols for chemical elements to complete the groups of words below. Words contained in a group use the same symbol.

1 O F _ _ N C E

   I N _ _ R N O

   _ _ L O N

2 R E C _ _ L

   _ _ L E G E D

   G _ _ L O W S

3 _ _ T I O N

   B A _ _ _ _

   A _ _ R C H Y

4 M _ _ N E T

   _ _ I L E

   B _ _

5 T _ _ O R Y

   _ _ A V Y

   B R E A T _ _

6

CROSS EXAMINE

In the science of detection nothing is straightforward. Avenues are explored, dismissed and then revisited when more information comes to light. This puzzle will take you down many avenues. There are three options given for each answer. There will be a lot of to-ing and fro-ing as you search for the correct solution. Only one of the three words will fit in each case and there is only one way to complete the grid. We give you a one word start.

ACROSS

8 Almanac * Ammonia * Arsenic
9 Taper * Topic * Viper
10 False * Solid * Solve
11 Cranium * Diagram * Problem
12 Keys * Ways * Wise
13 Heighten * Threaten * Tungsten
16 Deceased * Recorded * Reformed
18 Jade * Jail * Jury
21 Chained * Learned * Yearned
23 Asked * Askew * Faked
25 Skill * Steal * Wheel
26 Gambler * Rumbled * Similar

DOWN

1 Gems * Laws * Lies
2 Employ * Faulty * Guilty
3 Clues * Index * Snout
4 Acid * Axed * Gold
5 Arrange * Stealth * Strange
6 Spirit * Spooky * Sprite
7 Chemical * Criminal * Infernal
12 Wariness * Weaponry * Wireless
14 Owe * Urn * Use
15 Warning * Wrestle * Wrongly
17 Caught * Chased * Hoaxes
19 Alibis * Alkali * Upkeep
20 Enemy * Harms * Haunt
22 Date * Digs * Rage
24 Bury * Dank * Dark

7

WHAT'S YOUR POISON?

The cryptic clues below should help you track down the most Victorian of murder weapons, poison. At one time poison was untraceable but scientific advances changed all that. What can you uncover?

1   Eric's an unorthodox killer.

2   Give Nancy an ideal weapon for protection.

3   Fatal window blind not used during the day. (Two words)

4   Brother's headgear in garden danger.

5   Border fastening not to be tampered with.

8

FOOTPRINTS

Here are six pairs of boots. The individual footprints A to D were taken from the slimy mud at the scene of the crime. Which boots from 1 to 6 are not linked to the crime from the evidence shown?

CHAPTER FOUR

STORMING THE CITADEL

Scotland Yard has been welcoming remarkable female recruits for the last one hundred years; these women have brought ingenuity, knowledge and expertise to the Yard while simultaneously battling against the misogyny and the stereotypes inflicted upon them. Their work has been essential, and innovative, and naturally continues to be so today.

Nonetheless we can still imagine female police constables and female detectives standing out as the minority in police stations, tolerating with gritted teeth the antediluvian sexism of their male colleagues. This has been the engine of many popular television dramas, from *Prime Suspect* to *Juliet Bravo*; the idea that in a rough tough world of ruthless criminals, crimes had to be solved and thwarted by equally hard-bitten, punch-happy males. Women might be effective on the 'softer' stuff, but when it came to the gunpoint raids, the wage robberies, and the gang warfare, ladies would not be able to cope with such macho challenges.

It is true that it took some years to achieve equality; but the fact that today Cressida Dick is Commissioner of the London Metropolitan Police shows that the force is now adapting with the twenty-first century. As such, the puzzles in this section are inspired by the women of the Yard and the skills that make them indispensable.

The story of women at Scotland Yard is in some ways the story of modern Britain itself; a kaleidoscope of changing attitudes and assumptions, not only about wrongdoing, but about how best to deal with and prevent further crime. In 1916, at the height of the First World War, there were suggestions that with so many thousands of men out in the trenches it was time for Scotland Yard to consider widening recruitment. The popular press was aghast. 'Is there any possibility of women being employed as police constables?' enquired a reporter from the *Daily Express*. A Yard spokesman replied crisply: 'No, not even if the war lasts fifty years.'

Yet just weeks before the First World War ended, the Yard changed its mind and organised its first female intake. That is, official intake – several years beforehand, there had been Voluntary Women Patrols. They were set up in response to the press spreading fear about the wellbeing and motives of young ladies disporting themselves near army barracks and troop trains at railway stations. Thanks to the popular press, there were also (misplaced) fears that young ladies were being kidnapped and sold into the white slave trade.

In 1919, the number of policewomen was extremely modest, totalling around 112 (out of a force of about 15,000). There was one Superintendent, Sofia Stanley, one assistant Superintendent, ten patrol leaders and one hundred patrols. And the women on the beat could not be referred to as 'constables' but rather as 'Women Patrols'; the men of the Yard made sure they occupied a twilight area in the hierarchy. Nor were they actually given the power of arrest. When apprehending criminality they still had to turn to their male colleagues, in whom authority was vested. Despite this, they received full police training, including foot drill, first aid and police duty. Among these recruits were Grace Russell, Patty Alliott and Lilian Wyles.

In 1921, promoted to Inspector, Lilian Wyles managed to persuade the Criminal Investigation Department (CID) to allow women to take statements in cases involving sexual assault. Her insight was that it was not merely for the good of the traumatised victims, but also would serve the legal processes better. Having prevailed, Inspector Wyles then saw that women constables were given specialised training in taking statements, a progressive development in an age not widely noted for progress.

At this time, Scotland Yard was still very much ahead of every other police force – the number of female recruits elsewhere in the country could be counted on one hand – but by 1922, with the men long returned from the war, there was new pressure to disband the Yard's Women Patrols. First of all, there were budget cuts needed and these women seemed like a prime target, and second there were those who argued that it was now time to make the police an exclusively male preserve once more. In the House of Commons, Edward Shortt MP declared that 'policemen's wives' could do the work of the women constables. There were, of course, others who argued powerfully that this would be a disgracefully retrograde move. Among them, most prominently, was the MP Lady Astor, who argued that police officers did not marry on the basis that they wanted their spouses to patrol the streets.

The numbers were squeezed but women were not completely driven out of Scotland Yard and after the cuts, numbers began to rise again slowly. The principle of women in the force proved irreversible and in 1923, female police were at last given the power of arrest. On top of this, they were finally allowed to be referred to as constables. From here there was no turning back.

The London of the 1920s was a city of industrial mist and glowing neon. Damp West End pavements reflected the pink and green lighting of the more fashionable and louche streets. Though progress had been made, women were still held back from policing the rougher side of crime; the organised gangs, the mysterious murders. As the decade wore on, it became clear that female constables were being assigned largely to crimes of a domestic nature and by 1933, all juvenile cases were being routed through the women's branch. In one sense, this is a display of obvious sexism, yet it is also worth noting that this move possibly indicated a new kind of understanding about the roots of crimes committed by children, and how they should be dealt with. In the Victorian and Edwardian age, the accent was on fierce punishment, but by the 1930s the overbearing authoritarianism had given way to something a little more nuanced, a sense that some chaotic family backgrounds meant that many children never had a chance to pick the right path. This was the precursor to the 1990s vow from Shadow Home Secretary Tony Blair to be 'tough on crime, tough on the causes of crime'. For some female recruits in those early days, there was that driving sense of the possibilities of not merely solving but actually preventing crime.

Dorothy Peto, who had originally intended to be a novelist, joined the police properly – after an unofficially recognised stint with the Birmingham force – in 1927 and her commitment and expertise led to her becoming the first official woman Superintendent in 1930. Her strong emphasis on working with families was an important corrective especially in a decade where inner-city living conditions for the poor seemed to be getting worse rather than better.

However, the path to a detective career that was every bit as fulfilling as those open to men seemed far off. In 1931, any woman constable who got married was required to resign immediately. Unfortunately, this was not unusual; any woman in any profession was expected upon marriage to concentrate on making a home. It was some years – and another war – before such attitudes began to be relaxed. In any event, in the 1930s, numbers of female recruits were still very low but the outbreak of the Second World War in 1939 changed all that again.

It was the post-war years that saw women finally inducted as detectives, as well as constables. And in 1947, Detective Sergeant Alberta Watts was awarded the King's Police Medal for outstanding bravery. In the murky mists of night-time Tooting Common, in south London, there had been a number of attacks on women who had had their handbags stolen. DS Watts volunteered herself to act as a decoy and sure enough, in the thick fog, she was suddenly hit from behind. As she recovered herself, the assailant grabbed the bag from her shoulder, wrenching her arm and causing her to fall to the ground following which, with some apparent difficulty, she and a male colleague were able to subdue the attacker.

A few years later, in another south London borough, George Medals were awarded to two female officers: Kathleen Parrott and Ethel Bush. Parrott had been investigating sinister and terrifying attacks that were being carried out along a quiet cut-through path, and one evening she was confronted by the assailant, who struck her about the head with a length of log. Despite being hurt, she managed to rip the mask from the man's face and her testimony was invaluable in the later identification.

A short while after this, Ethel Bush, in uniform, was patrolling the area when she saw a man loitering suspiciously. With speedy presence of mind, she raced back to the station, changed into civilian clothes, and made her way back to the Fairfield Path. This was extraordinarily brave; to act not merely as a decoy but with a high chance of being seriously attacked. And in the darkness, the attack came. But this time, there were reinforcements and the assailant – a 29-year-old labourer – was apprehended and convicted.

It was 1957 when women were promoted to the role of Detective Inspector, and the first to be selected were Shirley Becke and Barbara Kelly. Shirley Becke went on, by 1969, to become the first woman Commander in Scotland Yard. Meanwhile, the first women in the Flying Squad (the branch of the Metropolitan Police dedicated to investigating serious large-scale robberies) joined in 1959, and Sislin Fay Allen, the first black woman police officer, was recruited in 1968. Fay Allen had been a nurse, but that all changed when one day she saw a recruitment advertisement in the newspaper. After passing the exams and the medical, she was posted to Fell Road police station in Croydon. She later said: 'I can remember one friend said, "oh they wouldn't accept you, they don't accept black people in the force", and so I said, "well, my dear, I've got news for you."' She recalled that her first days out on the beat were 'daunting' but 'after a while, the stares soon passed'. A trickier prospect on her first day was escaping from newspaper reporters. She was later transferred to Scotland Yard to work at the Missing Persons Bureau; then in 1972, she and her husband and children moved to Jamaica because of family commitments. Fay Allen joined the police force there, but remained an inspirational figure back at the Yard, paving the way for large numbers of recruits from a variety of backgrounds and heritages.

Broadly, however, slow progress was made in bringing female detectives to the fore due to the age-old assumption that policing and detecting were somehow not women's work. For a very long time, even the truncheon issued to female officers was much smaller and daintier than the model issued to men. While Lilian Wyles had been among the very first to challenge all the tokens of ingrained sexism (and indeed, her subsequent book about her life in the Force was published by Faber and Faber in the 1940s), figures such as Shirley Becke, who joined up in the Second World War, were every bit as admirably tenacious and, like a long relay race, succeeded in pushing out further.

Brought up in the leafy west London area of Chiswick, Shirley Becke had already, in the mid 1930s, decided to swim against the tide as a young school leaver; she was determined to follow her father and brother and become a gas engineer. When she presented herself at the local technical college the recruiter assumed that she had accidentally walked into the wrong room. 'We have never enrolled a girl before,' he told her. 'You have now,' Becke replied. And she applied herself to the course with energy. Five years later, she was one of the very few women engineers to work in a gas showroom. Then war came. And in 1941, she signed up to join the police.

During the black-outs, the streets of London were impenetrably dark and this necessitated female as well as male officers to be taught the fundamentals of self-defence. Becke's male colleagues were initially opposed to her joining patrols through the rougher districts at night. But she was insistent. As the war ended, Becke had acquired enough experience to join the CID.

And among the blitzed ruins of that post-war city, there were a surprising number of crimes to solve and gangs to thwart. In the foggy autumn of 1945, a gangster referred to as 'Russian Robert' was found dead in his car in one of the seedier corners of Bayswater. He had been shot in the back of the head. A gangland hit meant the leads were tenuous; and one such thin lead suggested that two named suspects – who could not be traced – might have been staying in a boarding house just to the south of Paddington Station. But how to track down such shadowy figures?

Shirley Becke applied herself to the problem and found the solution. She dressed up in plain civilian clothes and knocked on the doors of all the boarding houses near the station. She explained to the landlords and landladies that her fiancé had left her, and that she was 'in trouble', and thus needed to find him urgently. She described this fiancé (from the descriptions she had of one of the suspects) and eventually, one woman, clearly sympathetic, told her that she had seen the gentleman in question, and knew a little of his new whereabouts.

This was all she needed. Both suspects were swiftly tracked down and the murder of 'Russian Robert' was solved. In 1948, Shirley Becke was promoted to the rank of Detective Sergeant.

Operating out of the police station at Savile Row, just behind the brightly-lit splendour of Regent Street, Detective Sergeant Becke understood all too well the dangerous reality beneath the surface glamour. In the streets of 1950s Soho, she saw daily an array of call-girls and small-time mobsters; seedy clubs and even seedier drinking dens. Even though there were those at the time who romanticised this gaudy netherworld, Detective Sergeant Becke understood that it was always just on the edge of violence and cruelty.

Her experience made her valuable and in 1959, she was transferred from Savile Row to Scotland Yard, where she was the senior woman detective. By 1966, she was a chief superintendent, and in charge of a department specifically for female officers. She was adamant that Scotland Yard had to recruit more, advocating for equality before the sex discrimination legislation that would follow in the subsequent decade. By 1969, her title changed once more: she was now Commander Becke.

Yet this was still an almost preposterously male-orientated world. And perhaps her aims had not been terrifically helped by the publication of popular non-fiction books by women constables with titles such as *The Gentle Arm Of The Law*, which recounted police life in a selection of heart-warming vignettes. Becke's ambition was not only to eliminate the gender distinction but also to bring a new perspective and philosophy to the service.

The twenty-first century has brought significant changes in general social attitudes. In 2003, Sharon Kerr was appointed the first female head of Flying Squad, and in the same year, Janet Weller became the chief of Special Branch.

And in 2017, Cressida Dick was appointed the first woman commissioner of the Metropolitan Police. She began her policing career as a constable in 1983 and as well as experience across all departments, she also added an academic string to that bow, with a Master of Philosophy in Criminology from Cambridge. Indeed, what is most interesting about Dick is her keen intellectual interest in the criminal aspects of human nature; her aim to unlock the sometimes inexplicable with a range of different theories. But this has also been welded to a resourceful practicality in dealing with the most intractable criminal problems, such as gun crime. In 2003, as a Commander, she was in charge of Operation Trident, which tackled this specific issue across the capital. In addition to all of this, she has been vocal about the need for everyone to take pride in the city's diversity. It is fitting, in the centenary year of women in Scotland Yard, that there is now a call for the future force to be comprised of equal numbers of female and male recruits. What the pioneer women demonstrated was that – as in all other areas of life – there is a pressing need for problems, such as crime, to be approached from a variety of angles, and by people with a variety of experience. They show that those who uphold the law must reflect the broader society that they are protecting. And more than this: they demonstrate that different ways of thinking can find surprising and lateral ways into the knottiest crime enigmas.

1

FIND THE LADY

A mixture of male and female first names have been hidden in the word square below. All words are in straight lines and can go horizontally, vertically and diagonally. They may read forward or backwards. However, before you can root them out, you have to give the letters in the words below a twist, e.g the first word on the list is AID, but the name you seek is IDA. When you have found all the names there will be four letters remaining that have NOT been used. Those letters arranged in a certain way will spell out the name of a lady. Who is the lady you seek?

L	I	R	Y	C	N	E	I	L
Y	M	A	R	E	V	Y	A	I
D	D	A	I	L	R	H	N	A
I	N	M	R	E	T	T	D	M
A	A	S	H	I	A	A	R	Y
D	T	T	B	N	A	C	E	R
O	S	A	D	A	R	N	W	T
E	T	E	E	D	W	I	N	L
M	E	L	I	S	S	A	E	E

AID	AIMLESS	ANTS
ARMENIAN	DAILY	DANE
HABITAT	LINE	LYRIC
MAIDEN	MAIL	NAILED
RAVE	TERMLY	THREES
WARDEN	WIDEN	YACHT

2

OFF THE RECORD

Record keeping has always been an important part of police procedure. Accurate note taking is vital. The typing up of those notes was a key part of the process as well. Sadly in this case a member of the admin staff has made a few mistakes in the copy typing. There is just one incorrect letter in each clue. Can you tell which word is wrong, and put the correctly spelt word in the crossword grid?

ACROSS

7 The police officers pursued the shoplifters who had been at work in the detail park (6)

8 As the body was found in the forest, suspicion happened on a strong and sturdy tree filler (6)

10 He was a notorious lobster in a gang (7)

11 Just before tragedy struck at the wedding reception, the bride's father had proposed a roast for the happy couple (5)

12 They found the thin ringleader, the one who was in charge at the time (4)

13 The investigation into the theft of a number of beds took place outside a famous department snore (5)

17 When the police turned up to arrest Budgie Bird he was sitting on the perch in front of his house (5)

18 The officers were on their guard patrolling the soho back streets (4)

22 When the Royal Family meets lots of people, there is a need for the police to maintain crown control (5)

23 In order to avoid a long stretch in prison, the forger hid the false banknotes in the plastic waistband of his trousers (7)

24 Everyone agrees that all who cooperate in the community deserve braise at the highest level (6)

25 In difficult situations, nobody wants to be the beaker of bad news (6)

DOWN

1 The zookeeper, an expert on the private world, helped with the investigation (7)

2 In order to hunt down the horse rustlers, the riding staples were searched thoroughly by detectives (7)

3 Interpol were searching for the hijacker's berth certificate (5)

4 Eileen Dover, fraudster and fitness fanatic, was looking forward to going to the gym with her new leopard in her bag (7)

5 They all had to agree it was a typical croak and dagger story (5)

6 The grape had been cleaned out to find out what was lying in the ashes (5)

9 The bodyguards projected with great diligence everyone who was in their care (9)

14 Only the baldest people will be recognised as true heroes (7)

15 The hoofers could be heard from the boats on the river Thames (7)

16 The rogues tried to throw everyone off the scent by going to see a convert at the Royal Albert Hall (7)

19 The narrow timescale meant there wasn't a lot of slope for their activities (5)

20 The mural of the story is that crime doesn't pay! (5)

21 Modern detective work makes use of a great deal of loser technology (5)

3

DIARY DATES

Pearl Buttons, a renowned jewel thief, has vanished seemingly into thin air. On searching her Mayfair flat her diary was discovered with strange entries for two days of the week. With some clever deduction and a call to Interpol, Pearl was arrested. Where did she escape from them on Monday and where did they finally catch up with her on Thursday?

WEEK	
MONDAY	Monday – 7/4. 5/5/5. 5/5. Ring out more. Even silhouettes. The gold ran.
TUESDAY	
WEDNESDAY	
THURSDAY	Thursday – 11/2/5. 7/5/2/4. Dine at station there. Was not a foreign pile.
FRIDAY	

4

MULTI TASKING

Two circular grids. Two sets of quickfire clues. Each answer has five letters working from the outside inwards. All the answers in each individual circle grid end with the same letter of the alphabet. It's up to you to work out which answer goes in which circle. To get you started, answer 1 in grid A begins with the letter S. When each circle is complete the outer letters read clockwise will each spell out the name of a female detective; grid A is a real life one, grid B is a detective from the world of fiction.

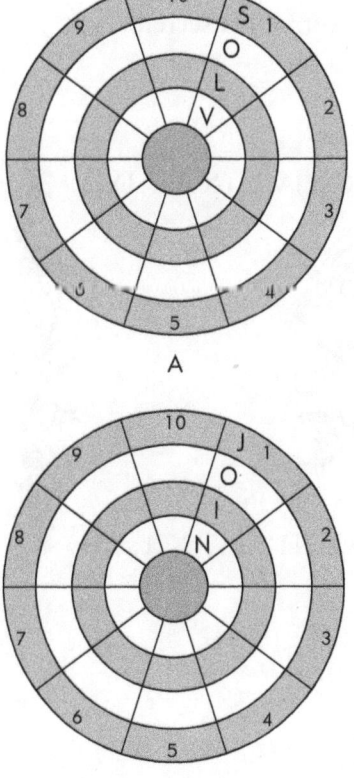

A

B

CLUES

1 Answer, explain * Where two bones meet

2 Rapidity * Representative

3 Hours of darkness * Nimble

4 Scoundrel * Precise

5 Power, strength * Conciliatory branch

6 Boldness * Watchful

7 Correct * Weapon

8 Run away * Sow seeds

9 Jumped * Planned course

10 Occasion * Extent

5

NEEDLEPOINT

Lady Rosa Bourbon is a world famous classical scholar. She is also an enthusiastic gardener and a very accomplished needlewoman, specialising in embroidery.

The other notable thing about Lady Rosa is her wealth. She has a collection of precious gems but she refuses to divulge their whereabouts, despite repeated requests from her nephews and nieces who are anxious to know where they are.

Lady Rosa's current piece of embroidery has a rose pattern at its centre, together with an elaborate border.

Do you get the point, or the needlepoint, of her secret?

6

LADIES DAY

Their menfolk may all be banged inside, but it doesn't stop the Walthamstow WAGS enjoying a day out. It's a trip to the races and the ladies are there decked in their new finery. Barbara Black, Betty Brown, Gill Green and Wendy White have all attended together in a group of four. A female Inspector from the Yard has kept a close eye on this group. She knows that each lady buys a new hat, new dress and new shoes for any major public event. The Inspector also knows that their clothes are in colours that match their surnames, so all the items are black, brown, green or white. Each lady has three different coloured items. No-one wears a colour that matches their surname. The hats, dresses and shoes are all different in colour.

The Inspector has heard that Betty bought a black hat and Gill had purchased white shoes for the racing trip.

A valuable cup vanishes on race day. Reports say that a lady in a green dress was seen leaving the tent where the trophies were stored.

Our lady Inspector was not on duty at the day of the races. She didn't need to be. She already knows who she will bring in for questioning. Who was the lady in the green dress?

7

PHONE LINES

One hundred years have gone by since women first joined the police force. Four friends recall the days when they became officers back in the 1970s. Not only did they have their own offices, but each had a dial telephone on their desk and an extension number of their own.

From the conversations below can you name each lady and match her to her own telephone extension number?

CHAPTER FIVE

COUNTRY HOUSES, LOCKED ROOMS AND STEAM TRAINS

One of the curious overlaps between real-life murder mysteries and the works of fiction that are devoured by the reading public every single year, is the recurrence of three archetypal settings. First, there is the attractive country house. Indeed, the country house murder mystery is a genre woven deep into the fabric of British culture, instantly identifiable anywhere around the world, and unfailingly popular.

The second setting very often lies within that country house, although it also turns up within office buildings, in medieval towers and sometimes in old-fashioned boarding houses. This is the locked room: that chamber in which the body is found, with the door mysteriously and bafflingly secured from the inside. This is such a staple of detective fiction that it is deemed to be a genre in its own right: the Locked Room Mystery. The best examples of these can be found in Chapter 8. But such enigmas have occasionally popped up in reality as well, as we shall see a little later with one particular case that unfolded in the East End of London in 1860.

The third setting that also turns up with remarkable regularity both in fiction and real life is the murder mystery that takes place on a train. In novelistic terms, the most famous is Agatha Christie's 1934 novel *Murder On The Orient Express* but there are so many recent examples, including *The Girl On The Train* by Paula Hawkins.

Here is the curiosity: these settings have in part risen out of real-life Victorian cases that seriously vexed Scotland Yard and completely mesmerised the newspaper-reading public. And so the puzzles in this section have a twist of that very traditionalist flavour; rambling country mansions with libraries and ballrooms, elegant sleeper trains crossing countries and continents, and a variety of logic challenges that require you to imagine being the detective approaching crimes that seem perfectly impossible.

In the wet summer of 1860, in a small Wiltshire village called Road, there was a murder that, in its own macabre and tragic way, set out the structure of what would become the classic mystery story. In the outside privy of a grand country house the body of a three-year-old child, Francis Savile Kent, was found. His parents, his siblings and the house servants were not only grief-stricken, they were also perplexed. The house had been securely locked that night and there was no sign of a break-in. Yet it could only be assumed that the killer had been an intruder because the other possibility, that the child had been murdered by someone within the household, was unthinkable.

Before the involvement of Scotland Yard, the local Wiltshire police worked upon another theory. They thought that the child's nursemaid, in whose room he slept, had a lover, and that in the middle of the night the child had awoken in a panic seeing the lover enter the room. The nursemaid and her lover had murdered the child to keep him quiet and their secret safe. In pursuit of this theory, the police found a bloody nightgown stuffed up inside a chimney. The idea was to keep it there but maintain a furtive watch over the room to see who would come and retrieve the incriminating evidence, and destroy it. The plan went wrong when one night, two constables got accidentally locked in the kitchen. When they got out, they found that the gown had gone and there was no indication as to who could have taken it.

The nursemaid, Elizabeth Gough, was arrested, but there was not even a scintilla of circumstantial evidence that could have pointed towards her. She was released shortly afterwards.

There was seething local speculation about another theory, again centring on Elizabeth Gough. It was thought that Gough was having an affair with the master of the house, Samuel Kent, and that it was he who had murdered the waking child during one of their trysts. This idea seemed to have been sparked by other rumours that Kent was a serial adulterer. Again, there was not a speck of proof. What it did show, however, was that a puzzling crime seemed a public invitation to open grand homes wide for all to peer inside, like some gigantic dolls' house, or the ever-popular game, *Cluedo*.

And so, the police concluded that greater expertise was needed. Inspector Whicher, a Scotland Yard detective who had already achieved a certain level of fame, was assigned to the case. He had solved other child murders, and used brilliant misdirection techniques in order to trap a gang of jewel thieves. Charles Dickens wrote of Whicher that his manner was that of a man 'engaged in deep mathematical calculations.' In travelling down to Road, it was the lot of Inspector Whicher to consider all possibilities, however hideous. And the responsibility for solving this ghastly mystery became enormous; for as well as the popular newspapers, there was serious scrutiny of the crime from politicians too.

This was the first great test of the perspicacity of Scotland Yard's still relatively new detective department, but this was also a time before any proper forensics. Inspector Whicher was forced on his wits to spot tiny logical inconsistencies and misplaced items that could point to the perpetrator.

The case brought with it exposure of the intimate history of the Kent family, the marriages and remarriages, the stepchildren. This was a case in which such knowledge could prove key, and yet – especially in the Victorian age when private domesticity was almost fetishized – the further agony this public scrutiny caused the family was intense.

Here, then, was the inspiration for generations of authors to come: a large house, with all the attractive comforts of wealth; a family that is serene and well-ordered on the surface, but with a less than serene history; loyal servants who witness in silence the private passions of the household. Added to this is the sense that the grand house becomes a hermetically sealed community. So much so that when it is locked up securely at night, there is no chance that whatever happens within can be blamed upon outside forces.

Therefore, the detective faces many challenges; he has to disentangle personal secrets, solve the logical puzzle of the house layout, and comprehend how a murderer might move undetected, concealing any trace of bloodstains that would otherwise incriminate them.

One of Inspector Whicher's insights, for instance, revolved around the routines of the household laundry, not knowing of the previous bungle involving the nightgown. Yet he was subliminally aware that some item was missing, like an itch at the back of his mind. Meanwhile, for the family, there was that slightly uncomfortable sense of dirty laundry both real and metaphorical being examined.

The other intriguing strand of the case reflected less in fiction but key to the public's perception of Scotland Yard detectives as the years wore on, was that of class. The Kents, as well-to-do upper-middle-class people, were (as the old phrase went) the social superiors of Inspector Whicher, who hailed from humbler roots in Camberwell, south London. From the start, there was a public fascination for the idea that a man of working-class stock could exert his will on a grand figure such as Samuel Kent.

But perhaps there was also a public sense that Mr Whicher's perceptions might be distorted a little by this reverse of power because his theory, upon which he made his arrest, was one that the reading public did not care for. The Inspector, after careful reflection on his conversations with all members of the household, had a growing conviction that the murderer was the little boy's older step-sister Constance. He had been alerted to suggestions of tension between the 16-year-old girl, her father and her stepmother; the mother of the little boy.

Constance was arrested, but without the nightgown, there was not even any circumstantial evidence. Mr Whicher's case collapsed, and with it – temporarily – his reputation. The newspaper reading public recoiled from the idea that a charming 16-year-old girl could commit such an unthinkably savage act. This was some years before Freud, and the idea of the unconscious.

But Inspector Whicher had been right, and Constance Kent eventually confessed to a High Anglican priest five years later, before handing herself over to the authorities. Now, of course, there would be a great deal of focus upon her mental health and surprisingly, even back then, there was some judicial understanding in that direction. There might have been those who would have expected Constance Kent to hang and indeed the original sentence was the death penalty. But this was quickly rethought with the judge and the authorities wisely revising their impulsive reaction. Instead, she went to prison, and twenty years later she was released. Upon gaining her freedom in 1885, aged 41, she emigrated to Australia to join her brother William who had moved there some years beforehand.

According to award-winning author Kate Summerscale, who explored the case so vividly, there was a terrible secret shared between these two close siblings. Constance had taken the weight of the responsibility for the murder completely on to her own shoulders when in fact the crime had been committed by both of them. Constance Kent lived until 1944, dying at the age of one hundred. Even by then, the case was alive in public memory, and ever more so, not just for the ghastly murder, but also for the element of class conflict that could not reconcile the seamy suspicions of a working-class police detective with the graciousness of an upper-middle-class 16-year-old girl.

Curiously, that same dismal summer of 1860 saw another real-life murder case, this time in East London, that provided a template for many fictional mysteries thereafter. The slaying of a wealthy, miserly and thoroughly unsympathetic slum landlady in her own rather smart and secure house was notable because no one could understand how the killer could possibly have got in. This was the prototype Locked Room Mystery. And it was – as we shall see – a story that captured the imagination of the creator of Sherlock Holmes. For within it, Arthur Conan Doyle detected the strong possibility of a miscarriage of justice.

Mary Emsley was a 70-year-old widow who owned countless squalid properties all over the East End of London, near the docks. By contrast, her own three-storied house near the elegant Victoria Park was pristine and spacious with a pleasant back garden big enough for pear trees. Mrs Emsley lived alone and unlike her neighbours she had no domestic staff other than a lady who came by on Saturdays to clean. More than this, though gregarious during the day, Mrs Emsley refused to allow anyone into her house after sunset. And anyone who knocked on the door after hours would face a full interrogation from the widow, leaning out of her first-floor window.

Her garden – and the neighbouring gardens – were enclosed in a square of houses. The only way into them was through one of those houses. And Mrs Emsley was careful about locking up at night. She also refused to keep much money in the house, ensuring her takings from rent were deposited with the landlord of the pub around the corner, prior to being taken to the bank. Some of this rent she collected herself; the rest she left to her trusted property managers.

So how then could the police have been greeted with such a scene of horror one grey morning in August 1860? One of her worried employees, having not seen the old lady for days, alerted her solicitor, and he in turn alerted some local constables. None of the neighbours had seen her come or go, or seen anyone else approaching the house. The thought was that Mrs Emsley might have taken ill.

There was no way in through the front door, no-one had spare keys. So, making their way through a neighbour's house, the solicitor and the police climbed into her back garden, and they found the back door of the house open.

Concern gave way to foreboding. They found the old lady in her lumber room, face down, holding a roll of wallpaper. The walls around were spattered red. Someone had smashed the back of her head in.

The hideous ferocity of the crime was one thing, but the only clue left behind was a boot-print, made in blood on the landing. There was nothing to suggest how the killer got into the locked house – or indeed got out again.

Because of the old lady's unkindness to so many of her East End tenants, any suggestion of arrears and they were evicted quite without pity, there was no shortage of suspects. But Scotland Yard, and the Home Office, thought there might have been more to it than some act of furious revenge. For the point was that Mary Emsley had been dazzlingly rich and there was the possibility that the culprit might have been rather closer to home.

Mrs Emsley had been married twice, she had lost a child very early and had no more, but she had several nephews. One was a soldier in Portsmouth who Scotland Yard described as having 'a very bad character', chiefly because of his habit (before her murder) of writing to other family members asking if the old lady was dead yet.

Added to this were two stepdaughters from her second marriage, and their husbands. Their late father Samuel Emsley had made a vast amount of money from corset-making, and so they were comfortably provided for. But Mary Emsley, most unusually for the time, had kept all her own financial dealings completely separate from her husband. The question that occurred to Sergeant Thornton at the Yard was: who stood to inherit the old lady's vast wealth? She had left no will of any kind, so was the murder perhaps prompted by her reluctance to name benefactors?

As with the Road case, the Mile End Murder became a newspaper sensation across the country. And it seemed speedily solved after an apparent attempt by one of Mrs Emsley's property managers to frame a colleague for the killing with an incriminating package of small items taken from her house. The package in question was hidden in an alcove behind Walter Emm's house, with a man called James Mullins leading the police to it. Yet it was gimlet-eyed Inspector Thornton who spotted that the string that held the paper package together was the same as those lacing the boots of James Mullins.

Inspector Thornton was certain he had his killer. And the fact that James Mullins, who had worked with Mrs Emsley for a year, was himself a former policeman pensioned out of the force in disgrace, appeared to add weight to Thornton's theory. This was an intelligent man, reduced to obeying the whims of an unpleasant old lady, and in his frustration he had caved her head in.

Mullins protested his innocence consistently. But the jury found him guilty. He was hanged at Newgate, in front of a crowd of 30,000 people. There are still many questions concerning the safety of this conviction: because even though Mullins had done a very wicked thing by trying to frame another man, it was clear to many that his motivation for doing so was the substantial financial reward that had been offered by the step-family of Mrs Emsley. In 1860, the £300 offered was a life-changing sum, equivalent to about £35,000. Mullins might also have been convinced – as a former policeman – that he had solved the crime, and that Walter Emm really was the guilty party. In addition to this: the evidence that was gathered against Mullins himself was described by the judge as circumstantial. Mullins would have known the old lady had no valuables kept in the house. So, what would he have gained by killing her?

And more importantly, how did he get in? The old lady never opened her door to anyone after sunset and since her watchful neighbours had seen nothing untoward in the day, she could only have been murdered at night. Although Mullins was one of her more reliable employees, she would never have tolerated his presence in candlelight. This element of the locked house was to be refined by countless authors; not least by Sir Arthur Conan Doyle. His early Holmes adventure *The Sign of Four* is a fine example of the locked room sub-genre. But in this real-life instance, he was troubled by the conviction and execution of Mullins.

Writing for the *Strand Magazine*, he brooded upon the timing of the murder and the inconsistencies of the case persecuting Mullins. Conan Doyle himself did not speculate any further, save to conclude that the conviction was unsafe. But the implication of his reasoning was that the killer was a confidant of Mrs Emsley, one with whom she was socially at ease. Someone so familiar that the neighbours would scarcely have noticed his presence at her door. And more than this, the killer would have had to have stayed in the house all night, and throughout the following morning.

Even with all the doubts, the murder was deemed sufficiently ghastly for a waxwork of James Mullins to be placed in the Chamber of Horrors at Madame Tussauds. Meanwhile the sergeant on this case, Richard Tanner, was promoted, and several years later as a Detective Inspector he was assigned to a gruesome and perplexing railway mystery that again seized the national imagination. For this was the first murder ever committed on a train.

It was the 9.45 p.m. Fenchurch Street to Chalk Farm line, a service running through new middle-class suburbs in east and north London in a loop. A 70-year-old chief bank clerk called Thomas Briggs boarded the train and sat in one of the train's first class compartments. He was travelling to his home in the leafier part of Hackney. The journey was short, a matter of twenty minutes; viaducts over the cramped, dark housing of Stepney thence heading north towards more prosperous locations.

At Hackney Wick station, just a little after 10 p.m., two gentlemen boarded the train and walked into the same first-class compartment. In the carriage gaslight, they could see a number of curious dark moist patches on the seating and the walls. There were pools on the floor. There were also some discarded items lying about: a walking stick, a leather bag, and a black felt hat. Very quickly, the men ascertained that the dark moisture was blood. At the next station, they alerted the train guard and other staff.

As arrangements were quickly being made to isolate the carriage, a train running in the opposite direction came to a very sudden halt between Hackney and Bow, on a stretch of line fringed with terraced houses. The train's stoker and driver had seen a body on the side of the tracks. At that point, Thomas Briggs was still alive, though unconscious. He had apparently been attacked, then hurled from the train.

Briggs was carried to a nearby pub, where a doctor attempted to revive him with stimulants. It was to no avail; and anyone gazing upon the extent of his horrific head injuries would not have been surprised. His skull had been cracked. Thomas Briggs was borne to his home a few streets away. And there, not long afterwards, he died.

Events must have happened as the train had been speeding from Bow up to Hackney, and the two stations were barely five minutes apart. The police were swift and decoupled the carriage in question from the rest of the train and it was taken to sidings at Bow. Meanwhile, it was ascertained that certain items had been stolen from

Mr Briggs, specifically his gold watch, with gold chain and a pair of gold eyeglasses.

It could not be known precisely where Mr Briggs's assailant had boarded or indeed alighted but what did seem certain is that a robber had beaten him brutally, stolen his valuable belongings and then pushed him on to the tracks. Inspector Tanner of the Yard was swift to see the one anomalous detail that stood out in its oddness. The hat that had been found in the carriage did not belong to Mr Briggs. His distraught family were absolutely certain of it. So, if it did not belong to him, was it possible that after the murderous assault, his attacker had picked up the wrong hat and disappeared into the night with it?

The mystery gripped the public because here was a confluence of two sources of unease; the possibility that violence could strike anyone in the rapacious city and the occasionally unsettling nature of the railways themselves. A dim, gaslit carriage on an especially dark evening, stations near the black expanses of the Hackney Marshes, respectable and well-to-do gentlemen and ladies suddenly finding their first-class worlds invaded by malevolent ruffians.

For Inspector Tanner, there were two trails to follow: the hat, and the stolen gold watch and chain. A label inside the hat revealed it to have been made in a shop in Marylebone. Meanwhile, in response to hefty publicity, a cabman called Matthews and a jeweller with the rather striking surname of Death, came forward. The trails were leading back to a young man of German heritage called Franz Müller. Various people, including his landlady, could identify the distinctive hat. And he had been to Mr Death the jeweller to exchange a gold watch and chain. In addition to this, Müller had been paying romantic visits to the daughter of the cabman, who saw him with the gold chain.

Unlike the Mullins case, there seemed to be no ambiguity, especially as Inspector Tanner discovered that the young man had already made his escape. He was, the Inspector ascertained, on board a sailing ship to America that had embarked a day or two previously. Sail was cheaper than steam, but steam was faster than sail. Inspector Tanner had a brainwave.

He and his assistant Sergeant Clarke made their way to Liverpool and from there embarked upon a much faster steam ship to New York. Their voyage took three weeks, and Müller was still at sea when they made land. From there, it was a question of interception and then extradition. Müller was brought back, convicted and, just at the point when the noose was around his neck and before the trapdoor beneath him swung back, the young man told the priest: 'I did it.'

As a direct result of the case, railway companies felt under pressure to respond to middle-class unease because prior to this, there had been many other (non-fatal) robberies carried out on train journeys. Passengers in dim compartments had no way of raising the alarm. There were two innovations, one rather more long-lived than the other. Peep holes were drilled into the walls of compartments, so that if there were any curious noises from the adjacent compartment, passengers could look through to ascertain what was going on. These peep holes, however, were soon felt to be rather creepy in themselves, no-one much cared for the idea of being furtively spied on by strangers. The other innovation, though, was the emergency cord. One sharp yank and the train driver would bring the locomotive to a halt, while the guard investigated.

This was not the last railway murder, though. For instance, at the turn of the century, a signalman witnessed a blurred struggle on board a London to Brighton train and later the body of a finely dressed woman was discovered in the Merstham Tunnel – the murderer was her lover. Then there was the curious case of Arthur Mead in 1936, en route to Paddington Station. Several stops beforehand, the train guard passed through and thought that Mead looked extremely ill. So he had him taken off the train to be seen by a doctor.

The doctor very quickly found that the now barely conscious man had been shot. The weapon appeared to be a gun specifically for use on horses. In his dying breath, Mr Mead declared that a stranger had boarded and done this to him. Yet the logistics did not quite fit his story. No passenger could have boarded at the station where he had claimed because the train was not timetabled to stop there.

The truth was sadder, as forensic scientists established. Mead had had a troubled history of mental health and had used the gun on himself. No one knew why he had chosen to blame a fictitious assailant.

So this was how railways, country houses and locked rooms became essential staples in the general public's appetite for sensational whodunnits and thrillers. From Agatha Christie's *4.15 to Paddington* to her 1949 classic *Crooked House*, to the more recent *The Necropolis Railway* by Andrew Martin, these are settings synonymous with a certain kind of Englishness and they are mysterious locations that evoke fear and foreboding as much as they evoke the logic and detection of the Scotland Yard.

1

THE VILLAGE FETE

THE SCENE

The Inspector is spending a weekend away from the hurly burly of London life visiting his great aunt in the sleepy village of Much Snoring. On the Saturday afternoon the village fete is in full swing in the stately gardens of Snoring Manor. There are flower and produce stalls and all manner of contests including the jam making competition. Disaster strikes however, when local landowner and judge Miss Havitall is fatally poisoned after sampling some jam.

There are five suspects, Miss Chief, Miss Deeds, Miss Lead, Miss Place and Miss Takes, all of whom have made a different fruit jam, and more crucially, have all been at loggerheads with Miss Havitall for different lengths of time. The initial cause of these squabbles was the fact Miss Havitall had become chairman of different village societies in preference to all of these five.

Look at the clues given. When you find a piece of positive information put a tick in the grid. When you find a piece of negative information put a cross. Cross refer all the information you collect until you can find which lady made which jam, how long they have not been speaking to Miss Havitall and which society was the initial cause of the rift between them.

THE CLUES

1   The lady who made the apricot jam had aspired to be chairman of the Sewing Society. This wasn't Miss Place.

2   Miss Chief made the damson jam. She had not spoken to Miss Havitall for more than a year. The quarrel was not over the Gardening Society.

3   Miss Deeds was disappointed not to become chairman of the Bridge Society but she wasn't the strawberry jam maker. That particular lady hadn't spoken to Miss Havitall for 6 weeks.

4   Miss Takes missed out on becoming chairman of the Craft Society, whose election had taken place just 3 weeks previously.

5   The raspberry jam maker had not spoken to Miss Havitall for 5 years!

THE EVIDENCE

Only now can you and the Inspector use the evidence to pinpoint the murderess. Another judge had tried the raspberry jam with no ill effects. The Luncheon Society had now been disbanded and therefore was not a reason for murder. The quarrel must have been festering for a long time, therefore quarrels which had taken place a matter of weeks before could be dismissed.

So . . . who is the murderess of Much Snoring?

		JAM					NOT SPOKEN					VILLAGE SOCIETY				
		APRICOT	DAMSON	PLUM	RASPBERRY	STRAWBERRY	3 WEEKS	6 WEEKS	1 YEAR	2 YEARS	5 YEARS	BRIDGE	CRAFT	GARDENING	LUNCHEON	SEWING
NAME	MISS CHIEF															
	MISS DEEDS															
	MISS LEAD															
	MISS PLACE															
	MISS TAKES															
VILLAGE SOCIETY	BRIDGE															
	CRAFT															
	GARDENING															
	LUNCHEON															
	SEWING															
NOT SPOKEN	3 WEEKS															
	6 WEEKS															
	1 YEAR															
	2 YEARS															
	5 YEARS															

NAME	JAM	NOT SPOKEN	VILLAGE SOCIETY

2

TRACKING

A London train makes a journey in which there are five stops, with the fifth being the terminus.

It is suspected that stolen goods change hands during the journey of the last train each evening, with the middle carriage the likely place where activity takes place. The police are tracking the train and are keen to ascertain who was in the middle carriage throughout the journey.

On one night, five passengers in all travelled in the middle carriage. The railway staff at various stations are certain that there were always two people in that carriage. The second stop was the only station where no one got in or got out.

Mr Lawrence was the only person who never shares the carriage with Mr Peters. Mr Noakes boarded the train at the first stop. Mr Mason got in at a station further down the line than Mr Clarke.

Who was in the middle carriage throughout the journey?

3

WHERE THERE'S A WILL . . .

The reading of the last will and testament of a deceased person was a major event on country house estates. At Hardup House the family is present to hear the reading of Great Uncle Henry's will, which could be the solution to all their money problems.

The word WILL is the starting point in this puzzle, in space 1, and goes from the outer rim of the circle to the centre. All answers to the clues contain four letters and one letter changes in the answer in each move. The item which is inherited in the will is the answer in space 7, directly opposite space 1. What is it? We give you clues but they are in random order.

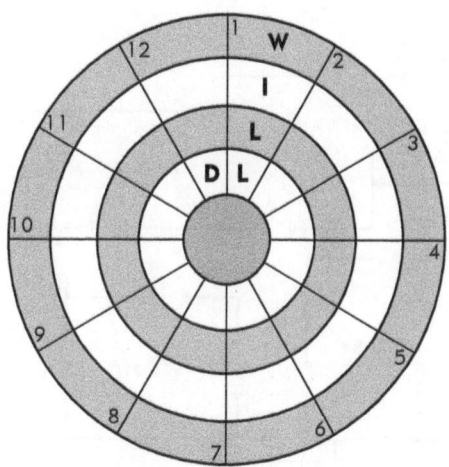

CLUES:

Decline in power or prosperity

Rich, natural fabric

Glower and scowl

Ledge by a window

Breeze

A financial institution

A great quantity or volume of an item

Untamed, feral

Source of misery or trouble

One bed on top of another

Drink produced from the fruit in a vineyard

4

MALDARK MURDERS

Captain Baggitt was staying at his favourite country house Maldark Hall. In the library he found a book chronicling a deadly murder trail at the Hall many years before. Intrigued about the victims on that fateful day, he tried to solve the mystery himself. Four people were murdered, each in a different room and with a different weapon.

Put these crimes in order, identifying each member of the household, where the crime took place and what the murder weapon was.

The murderer entered at the main entrance and did not retrace his steps. Captain Baggitt worked out the deadly route he had taken, room by room. Can you do the same?

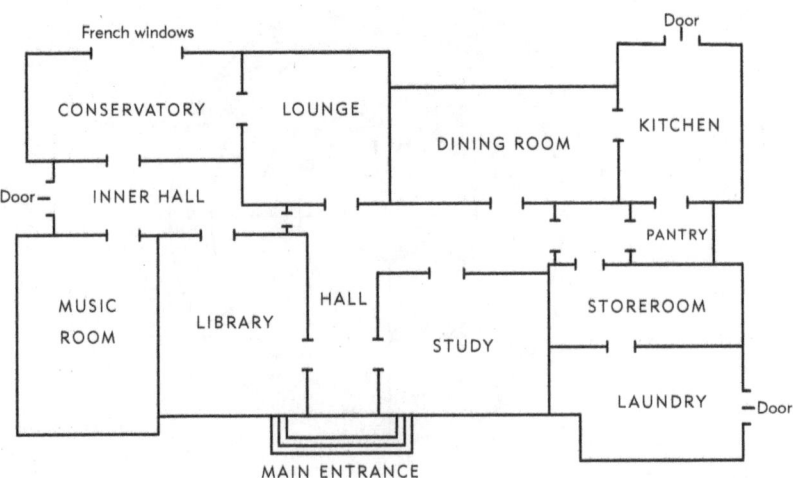

CLUES

1 Poison was administered in the crime which took place immediately before the murder in the conservatory.
2 The governess perished before the murder with the rope and the murder in the pantry.
3 The groom was murdered in the dining room. He was attacked with a candlestick.
4 The coachman was victim number 2.
5 The unfortunate housekeeper was not the person murdered in the library.
6 A pistol was used in the final crime.

5

AT YOUR SERVICE

The Chief Inspector has called at Moneybags Mansion, home of the eccentric Lord Moneybags. He is there in order to investigate the suspicious disappearance of the Head Gardener, along with a large amount of money, which had been locked in the safe.

'How many servants do you have here Lord Moneybags?' asked the Chief Inspector.

'Now let me think,' Lord Moneybags replied. 'I'm always forgetting so I have a special way of remembering which I will share with you. You are looking for the smallest number where the name of the number when written out in capitals is made up of the same number of straight lines as the number itself.'

How many servants did Lord Moneybags have?

6

LET OFF STEAM

In the heyday of steam trains, small rural branch lines criss crossed the British landscape. Your journey starts at the small rural station of Mouldsy. Find a route that calls at all 18 stations. Notmuch Appens is the final destination of the steam train. You can not go to the same station twice.

If you are in a Bradshaw mood, set off from Mouldsy as before but this time you can finish anywhere after visiting all 18 stations. Which stations can NOT be the final destination of a journey?

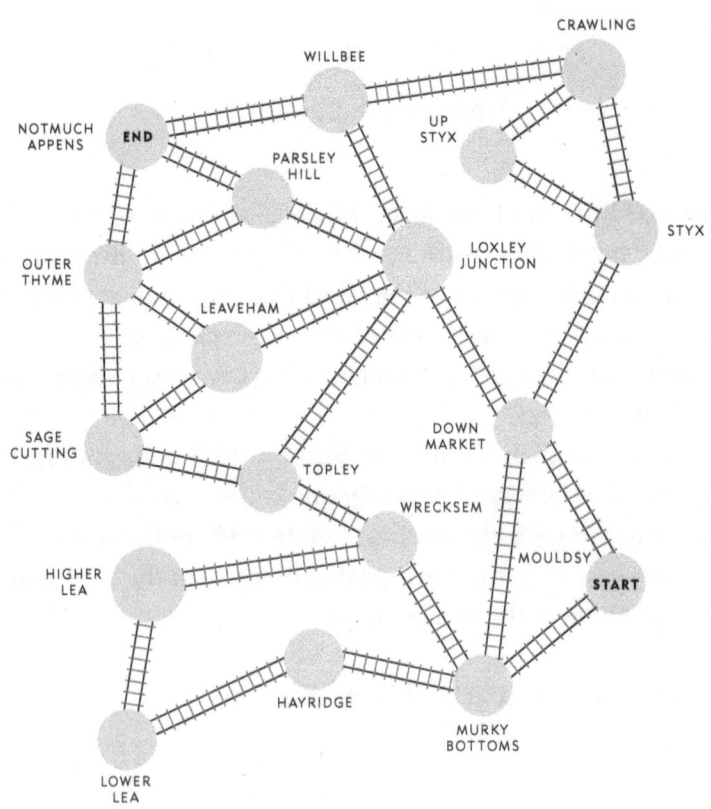

7

FARE'S FAIR

The new train company, London And Terminuses Everywhere, LATE for short, was based in the capital. It needed a quick and efficient way to establish tariffs for its journeys. Setting aside the usual criteria – fuel costs, staffing, distance and the like – it hit on an ingenious system.

Here is a list of its fares from London to different parts of the country:

RHYL – £4

FIFE – £6

TRING – £6

BRISTOL – £9

KING'S LYNN – £10

INVERNESS – £12

What was the logical – though totally impractical – basis on which fares were fixed?

8

HEDGE YOUR BETS

You have been summoned to Findem Hall to attend a top secret meeting. The rendezvous is to take place in the summerhouse situated at the centre of a maze of hedges in the magnificent manicured gardens.

The arrow points the way in. You have to find a path that runs between the tall, thick hedging and leads to the summerhouse . . .

The meeting starts in two minutes. Will you get there in time?

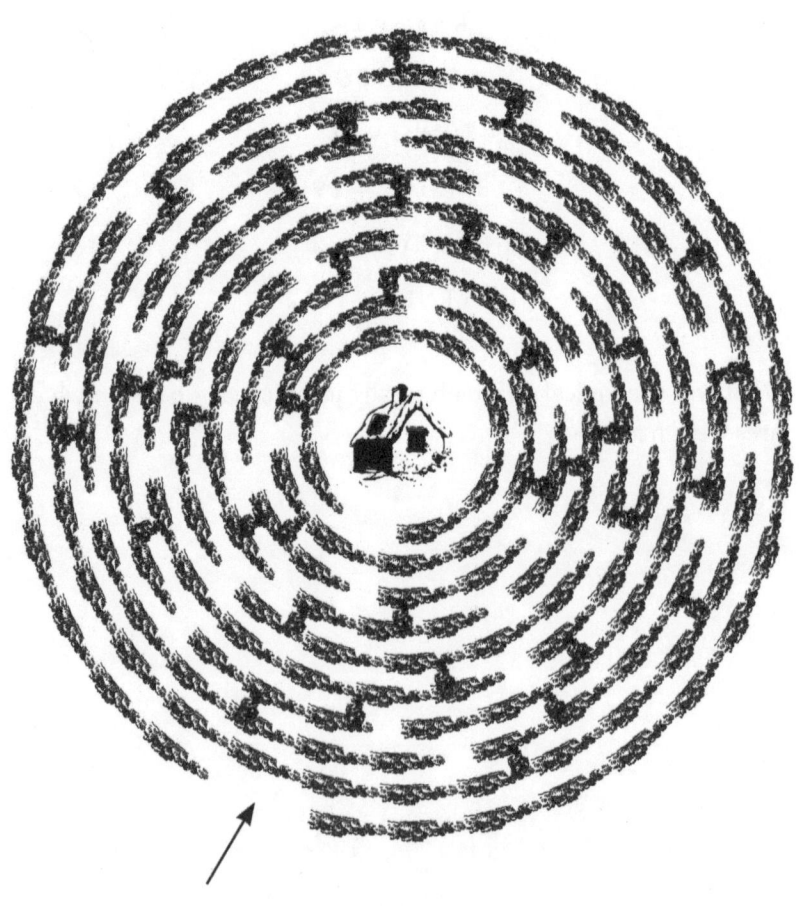

THE DIABOLICAL MASTERMINDS

There were some criminals who created specific difficulties for Scotland Yard not merely because of their elusiveness, but also because they were regarded by some as anti-heroes: figures who received a certain reluctant admiration from newspapers and the reading public alike.

Though the Metropolitan Police was the admired bulwark against forces of violence – the trusted bobbies on the beat – there was a type of crime that carried the thrill of escapist intrigue. This being the society jewel thieves who elegantly insinuated their way into the very finest Knightsbridge and Belgravia salons, and spirited away breathtakingly beautiful jewels.

These were the kind of stories that blazed across the newspapers and magazines of the 1920s and 1930s. And after the Second World War, the detectives of Scotland Yard had to deal with other less fragrant transgressors who also began to command a kind of social cult appeal. Most notably, certain London gangsters and hoodlums.

This public fascination with certain kinds of crooks has a very long history indeed, stretching back into the eighteenth century to the crimes of highwayman Dick Turpin and jailbreaker Jack Shepherd. These sorts of wrongdoers – who target the rich not with violence but amusing guile and subterfuge – have always given readers a vicarious thrill. From meticulously planned country house artwork heists to the daring and seemingly inexplicable cracking of impregnable safes, these crimes have caused a huge number of headaches for Scotland Yard. Nonetheless, they fed and continue to feed the wider popular imagination.

The puzzles in this section test your inner evil genius with safe codes to be decrypted, mazes of mansion corridors to navigate and guards and dogs to avoid. From the mathematical challenges of security systems to conceiving foolproof getaway routes, being a diabolical mastermind and outwitting Scotland Yard is not easy.

Although it might sound morally dubious to say so, society jewel thieves enjoyed a golden age in the 1920s and 1930s, and judging by the reports, Scotland Yard detectives themselves sometimes held them in a grudging awe. Especially striking was the 1930s criminal who became known to the public as 'Tiptoes'. Here was a thief who broke into expensive Mayfair apartments when the occupants were out or away, and as well as helping himself to jewellery and valuables, would leave his calling card written in lipstick on a mirror: 'Tiptoes'.

He was an operator who fearlessly stole across roofs, and silently forced windows open. A man who then sleekly slipped back into darkness. When, at last, he was apprehended by sharp-eyed detectives, it turned out that this suave acrobat was actually a rather timid young man from south London. Tiptoes was his more glamorous alter ego.

Tiptoes' youth was not an anomaly. Another criminal, 27-year-old George McRaigh was caught by Scotland Yard operatives in 1921 after a long career of jewel thefts. The detectives told the newspapers of McRaigh's fantastical life. He was 'a swell cracksman' (meaning terrifically good at opening safes), he 'mixed with the best society', 'dined at the smartest of hotels' and more than this he spent 'five pounds a day on champagne for his friends.' That five pounds went much further in 1921 than it would do today.

A few years later, a Scotland Yard source briefed *The Times* about the rise of the swanky criminal. 'The jewel thief is usually a "Raffles" type rather than Bill Sikes,' ran the report. (Arthur Raffles was a fictional gentleman burglar in a series of popular short stories written by E. W. Hornung; an elegant anti-hero who was driven to crime sometimes more by compulsion than any financial need.)

'He will frequent the best hotels, sit in the stalls at theatres, go to the best enclosures at race-courses. A thief who was recently caught,' the report continued, 'had beautifully manicured hands which he protected with lavender kid gloves, while his pocket-set of burglar's tools was enclosed in a neat leather case with chamois leather coverings for all the sharp-edged tools.'

Jewel thieves with impeccable dress sense and sharp wits continued to plague the aristocracy and those with great wealth. In 1946, the Duchess of Windsor, visiting England with the Duke and staying in a house borrowed from the Earl and Countess of Dudley – Ednam Lodge, in Sunningdale near Windsor – had £25,000 worth of jewellery (according to the Duke's estimate) stolen by a thief who had sauntered in through the front door. A friend of the Duchess, which most probably meant the Duchess herself, told the newspapers: 'The robbery took place at dusk on Wednesday evening while the Duke and Duchess were on their way back from London. No-one heard anything.'

The stealthy thief, not noticed by any staff or groundsmen, seemed to know exactly what he was after, stealing the black box containing the jewellery. Inspector Capstick was on the case and noted prints beneath the Duchess's window which showed how the criminal had left the house. A little later, the black box itself was found, discarded on a nearby golf course. Some jewels were left inside. The thief had made his careful selection, most probably based upon what he could sell through intermediaries without the pieces being instantly recognised, and escaped.

Nonetheless, the Yard persisted – and five years later in 1951 they made their way out to Windlesham Court in Surrey. They had had a tip-off from a source that some of the jewels had been buried in the grounds, presumably until the heat had died down and they could be retrieved and sold internationally. The police dug, but they found nothing. Possibly they were too late. One of the difficulties with this sort of crime was precisely that it was the opposite of passionate. These were near-military operations planned coolly, carried out with nerves of ice, and before the escape the criminal would take the greatest care to ensure all traces of his crime would vanish with his ill-gotten jewellery.

It was undeniable that there was an element of romance here, so long as the victims were sufficiently wealthy, and completely insured. This was certainly the case with the Duke and Duchess; the jewels had been insured for a six-figure sum. The theft of beauty will always be a blow, but the absence of any financial consequences, in the eyes of most newspaper readers, meant these cases were thrilling and exciting.

This is why reporting of such transgressions focused on the method, rather than the morality, of the thieves. In the early 1930s, amid the opulent mansions of Park Lane and Mayfair, a thief in full evening dress carried out an audacious robbery as an unwitting family and their servants went about their evening routines. The target was one particular piece: a necklace worth £40,000 (obviously many times that now), made of graduated pearls set in platinum and interspersed with diamonds. It belonged to the wife of businessman Mr W. Mosenthal, and was stored safely in her boudoir.

Mr and Mrs Mosenthal were downstairs and there were servants going about their business all over the house. It was just after 6 p.m.. Mrs Mosenthal went upstairs, and while she was in her boudoir, she realised the necklace was missing.

The police were called instantly and Scotland Yard detectives were at the house within minutes. They quickly fathomed three things. First, that there were witnesses outside who had not seen anything that appeared incongruous; second, a servant had seen a very elegantly dressed man climb into a car with several other less elegant figures; and third, whoever had taken the necklace clearly knew the layout of the house. How did he get in? It was possible this boulevardier had slipped in through the kitchen back door while the servants were bustling about preparing dinner. But Scotland Yard had another theory, too, that the crime had been so well prepared that the thief had a duplicate key for the front door. On this particular occasion, the theories were not sufficient to track down the languid thief but it did prompt other society hosts in the area to nervously tighten their own security. And since then, the Yard has built up a rather more impressive array of tools to outwit nefarious robbers.

These days there is of course a very much more extensive database (and not kept on cross-referenced cards, as in the old days), as well as formidable technological armoury, when it comes to apprehending jewel thieves. In the new world of CCTV and DNA, and with the invaluable element of strong international links, often the most debonair of thieves can be identified. Added to this, the security measures that the super-rich can take now rather outdo the modest precautions of the Duke and Duchess of Windsor.

Yet today there are other sorts of villainous masterminds who can beat the system. Figures who, throughout the years, have been very well known to the detectives of Scotland Yard, yet have somehow contrived to put themselves just beyond arrest, normally by employing proxies to carry out their nefarious work.

A few years before the advent of the publicity-hungry Kray twins (when Ronnie and Reggie were still in short trousers), the East End had other crime lords, including the prominent Jack 'Spot' Comer. Jack was known as 'Spot' because of a large mole on his face. Brought up in Jewish Whitechapel, Comer ran a variety of rackets, including illegal betting. By the late 1940s, Scotland Yard was well aware of Comer's illicit business concerns and occasionally their intelligence paid off handsomely and they managed to thwart some big operations. One such occasion, a 1948 raid on a goods warehouse at what was then known as London Airport, came to be known as 'The Battle of Heathrow'. The Yard were on the case, and officers from the Flying Squad were lying in wait as the villains tried to set their plan in motion. However, Comer was one step removed from the attempted heist, acting as a financier and strategist as opposed to active participant. It took a physical attack on a journalist to actually get him arrested. In that instance, the sentence was a £50 fine.

Comer's rackety concerns were rather badly hit by the rise of a former business partner, a determined and ferocious figure, called Billy Hill, a St Pancras-born Londoner who had been born into a family of criminality. He had essayed all manner of offences, from intimidation and violence to jewellery theft and protection rackets. He was a man permanently on the radar of the capital's detectives.

Billy Hill initiated gang warfare against 'Spot' while planning bigger and more daring crimes himself.

One involved an intricately planned central London postal van robbery in which Hill and his gang managed to grab £287,000 in cash (worth many millions now). The robbery had even been carefully rehearsed the Sunday beforehand in quiet streets. The gang manoeuvred their cars around a van to sandwich it and curious passers-by were told that they were making a film. The following year's hit Ealing black comedy *The Ladykillers* (1955) included a reference to the robbery. Prime Minister Winston Churchill did not find it a subject for levity, however, and in the days after the raid he demanded regular updates. Unfortunately for Scotland Yard, the gang was able to spirit itself away, most probably out of the country.

But the Yard knew very well that Billy Hill was the kingpin. He had served one prison sentence in the 1940s, after which he met and fell into a long lasting relationship with Gypsy Riley. She took his name and became Gypsy Hill (not in tribute to the wooded south London area that had been popular with eighteenth-century Romani people – although her first name *had* been bestowed by her mother because the girl was thought to have a Romany 'look' about her). Gypsy was soon to become a much sought-after figure by journalists who relished the colourful copy that she always provided. Rumour had it that on the postal van raid, she was one of the getaway drivers. She had a formidably mercurial temper and Soho nightclubs would clatter with flying chairs if she felt herself to be slighted. Following the postal van raid, and a gold bullion heist, the next Scotland Yard learned of Billy Hill was that he and Gypsy were in Tangier. Billy had bought her a sophisticated nightclub. They called it 'Churchills'.

There was an unavoidable fascination here, both for Scotland Yard and Fleet Street. A grudging acknowledgement that some criminal lives were irresistibly vibrant and glamorous. Even more maddeningly, and amusingly, Billy Hill decided to work on an autobiography, called with admirable brazenness, *The Boss of Britain's Underworld*. The book's proposition suggested that Hill had had a rackety youth but the gangs and the crime were now behind him. He held a book launch party in an expensive Soho restaurant and among the guests were journalists and policemen. Polite society, as expressed in the pages of conservative journals, shuddered. But before the grim and grotesque violence of the Kray twins and the Richardson gang, here was a figure who might have thought of himself as more of a rogue than a villain (even if the reality of maintaining control over Soho's criminals meant menacing people with knives).

Hill justified his own criminal rapacity by claiming it was a national characteristic. He had been fascinated by Walter Raleigh, Francis Drake, Clive of India and Captain Cook as a boy, and what else were they but thieves on a grand scale, sailing far off oceans and simply grabbing, plundering and looting anything that they desired?

By the 1960s, Billy Hill had edged himself into the realms of the dissolute upper classes. There were rumours that he was working with a very well-known casino near Knightsbridge that nightly saw titled aristocrats at the green baize tables. The rumour was that, by using a system of ingeniously tampered-with cards, the high-rolling aristocrats were being cheated out of legitimate winnings in crooked games, and the proceeds were being shared between Hill and the house. As with the jewel thieves of previous decades, here was the attractively transgressive idea that a working-class man might be able to fleece landed wealth. Again, there was little Scotland Yard's detectives could do about it.

Hill wore trilby hats and tinted spectacles, but Gypsy favoured expensive fur. In the 1960s, they became friends with the film actress Diana Dors. On their trips abroad to fashionable enclaves, Gypsy met Aristotle Onassis, second husband to Jackie Kennedy, and the artist Picasso. Billy Hill was always quite content to have held the self-bestowed title of the Boss of Britain's Underworld but even underworld bosses have to call it a day at some point. And in the 1970s, he retired from crime and devoted himself to taking his young son to the zoo and Madame Tussauds.

While it is true that there always have been, and always will be, some criminals who evade the grasp of Scotland Yard's brilliant detectives, over the years there have also been some who felt that they were above the law and far beyond the reach of the Yard, when in fact they could be hauled down with an immensely satisfying velocity. This was the case with Ronnie and Reggie Kray: two obvious sociopaths who throughout the 1960s somehow managed to lure celebrities into their spangled nightclubs, while they violently controlled the streets of London.

The Krays' empire was spread across the city with protection rackets, viciously enforced. Neither twin was shy about using guns. Their circle of closest associates was incredibly tight, and obviously a word against the Krays to the authorities could spell doom not merely for the 'grass' but his entire family. Nevertheless, from 1966 onwards, Scotland Yard were patiently on the case, infiltrating and monitoring. During this time, the Krays carried out two murders that they fully believed they would get away with. That of a small-time gangster called George Cornell, who was shot in the head as he sat in 'The Blind Beggar' pub in Whitechapel, and that of an associate called Jack 'The Hat' McVitie, who was stabbed in Hackney. Detective Inspector Leonard 'Nipper' Read was determined to outwit them, in spite of a criminal community that would never dare speak out, and the Krays were arrested in 1969. Their trial was a sensation. Ronnie Kray, a paranoid schizophrenic, was committed to Broadmoor hospital and Reggie Kray was sentenced to life in Maidstone prison. Scotland Yard 1; the Krays 0.

There are some other crimes that appear almost cinematic both in their scale and in their colour. One extraordinary attempted theft came in the year 2000 but happily, Scotland Yard's Flying Squad was there to thwart it. The target was the Millennium Star, a 200 carat diamond, almost priceless. It was located at a De Beers diamond exhibition at the Millennium Dome, just by the River Thames in Greenwich. The criminal plan: to use an excavator truck to crash through the wall of the Dome and ammonia and smoke bombs to knock out guards and security staff. A speedboat waited on the river to be used for the escape.

The Millennium Star was not the only prize the gang had their eyes on. The exhibition also featured a display of wildly valuable blue diamonds. The plot was months in the making and the Scotland Yard surveillance of it was equally patient.

The tip-off came from the Kent constabulary, who had been monitoring the three chief figures of the gang for some time. Scotland Yard had also come across the felons a few months previously, when they had attempted a security van heist in south London, in part using a lorry that was loaded up with Christmas trees as a weapon. The foliage of the trees disguised a big spike attached to the vehicle's chassis that was to be used as a battering ram. This plan had been narrowly thwarted by a random commuter who saw the (temporarily) empty cab of the lorry, noticed the keys left in it, and removed them, to stop anyone stealing the vehicle. Some weeks later, the gang tried again, and succeeded in jabbing the spike into the security van's doors. But on that occasion, a police car happened to materialise on the scene, and the putative robbers made a bolt for it down to the river where they escaped in a speedboat. From that point, they were ever more firmly on the radar.

The Yard had enough intelligence on the gang to take serious notice when the three key players visited the diamond exhibition a few weeks later. Caught on security camera, the men affected general interest in the exhibition. One had brought a home video camera and was taking shots of the jewels in their cases. The Yard shrewdly noted that a couple of further visits were made to the exhibition and also that each of these visits coincided with high tide on the Thames.

Linking up with Kent police, the Yard observed that one or two members of the gang were down at the coast learning how to use a speedboat. When the boat was brought up to London and moored opposite the Dome, the Yard thought it likely that the gang would strike.

Scotland Yard had of course notified De Beers and the Millennium Dome, and Operation Magician, the plan to thwart the raid, was every bit as spectacular as the planned crime itself. And at three o'clock on the morning of the planned heist, it was put into full operation. This meant not only a team of officers in the CCTV control room but also the substitution of all Dome staff, security and otherwise, for police officers.

As the criminals later averred, their plan was not to hurt anyone. Instead, they were going to bulldoze the Dome wall, race to the exhibition firing off smoke bombs, shoot a bolt gun at the reinforced glass of the exhibits, grab the diamonds and race to the speedboat to escape downriver in the direction of the estuary.

In reality, they succeeded only in smashing their way into the building; and beginning to break the glass. They didn't know that all the diamonds they were attempting to grab – from The Millennium Star downwards – were fake. And they did not even have a chance to get away with these as the police swooped in before the glass case had even shattered.

Meanwhile, on the river, the getaway speedboat was surrounded by water-borne police. Operation Magician was a complete triumph and as they were arrested, even the criminals seemed to show a little grudging admiration for the fleet-footedness of the Yard.

While it does not do to glamorise, the nature of a planned heist has just a note of romantic escapism about it. Even the conundrum of how anyone could hope to sell the Millennium Star – who would buy the world's most famous stolen diamond? – tugged at the imagination. Nonetheless, as one of the gang ruefully said, if they had managed to get the jewels and take off down the river, they would have had 'a blinding Christmas'.

The public appetite for reading about the plots of criminal masterminds never seems to diminish, sometimes to the exasperation of Scotland Yard veterans. The perpetrators of the 1963 Great Train Robbery, a violent heist in which over one million pounds was grabbed from a mail train in Buckinghamshire, were seen as the ultimate anti-heroes, with Buster Edwards, who succeeded in fleeing the country to south America, occasionally held up as a kind of popular folk hero. Even if the truth was that the robbery was brutal, leaving a coshed train driver with life-long injuries.

There was also the case of an elegant folk hero from a century before, described by Scotland Yard's Inspector John Shore as 'the

Napoleon of the criminal world'. Adam Worth blazed such a criminal trail in late Victorian London that he directly fired Sir Arthur Conan Doyle's imagination. Worth was an American who, as a very young man, had begun his swindling career throughout the American Civil War. After cracking open a safe in Boston, Massachusetts – and being thwarted by the detective agency Pinkertons who managed to track down his temporary hiding place for the loot – he fled the States and set sail for England. For a time, he travelled further, setting up an 'American bar' in post-Franco-Prussian-war Paris. Downstairs, this bar served drinks. Upstairs was an illegal gambling den. Any sign of the authorities, and the specially designed tables and chairs were folded and slotted into the walls and the floor.

Following this, Adam Worth (under the name Henry Raymond) came to London with his wife. He was determined to live in opulence, and move within fine society. As well as a flat in Piccadilly, he acquired a grand villa overlooking Clapham Common, then a very fashionable address. His manners and taste were so fine that he was ushered warmly into London's social whirl. But his criminal activities continued apace. From careful cons to safe-cracking, he generated a small industry of carefully calculated misdemeanours, while always insisting to his henchmen that no violence was to be used.

Inspector John Shore of Scotland Yard was alive with suspicion. He knew that the threads of a capital-wide web of crime led back to Worth. But Worth was always far too careful to ever allow any hint of an association with the crimes that he commissioned. Inspector Shore had his house watched day and night, yet still there was nothing that might be presented to his superiors as proof of wrongdoing.

But Worth could not always resist the adrenaline injection of carrying out a crime himself, and in 1876, he fixed upon a target. The luminously beautiful portrait of Georgiana, Duchess of Devonshire, painted by Gainsborough, had come on to the market. It was being held at the Bond Street art dealers Thomas Agnew and Son. Late one night, Worth and two associates broke into the shop and snuck away with the painting. The associates were eager for Worth to find a buyer, so they could get their financial cut, but Worth had fallen in love with the portrait. He did not want to be parted from it, so he paid them their dues, and kept it. He took ingenious precautions, such as having a false bottom fitted in his travelling trunk in which the painting could be hidden, but with so many subordinates, he was bound to be given away at some point. And indeed, when one of his henchmen, a man called Bullard, was jailed in Belgium, Worth's own nemesis came when he went over there to visit him. If Worth had simply confined himself to a simple prison visit, he would have been all right. Instead, having seen his friend, and faced with spending some leisurely hours in the city of Liege, Worth gave in to his old compulsions and staged a robbery – very badly. He was captured and the Yard's Inspector John Shore was there to assure the authorities that Worth's criminal history was vast and varied.

Although he had been caught red-handed, Worth simply denied everything else the Inspector accused him of. He would confess to this particular robbery, but everything else, he averred, was a tissue of lies. He served seven years in a Belgian prison and was then a free man once more.

The wider point of Worth's flamboyant tale is that a few years after his arrest, Sir Arthur Conan Doyle seized upon him as a model for the master criminal James Moriarty. Worth was the real-life strategist who gave inspiration for the fictional diabolical mastermind who left no trace, no clue, no sign. Moriarty outfoxed the authorities in Europe and America, and could only be out-thought and out-witted by Sherlock Holmes.

In reality, the law catches up with even the most amusing of serial transgressors, and, though we can admire the wit and determination involved in pulling off these lighter crimes, we will always be grateful for the sharp minds of Scotland Yard who eventually – after an entertaining chase – succeed in catching them.

So here then is a selection of puzzles that puts you in the shoes of the roguish transgressors, rather than those who catch them; tests of nerve and calculation designed to measure the extent of your inner diabolical mastermind. After all, as much as it takes logic to defeat crime, it also takes mental discipline to map out grand felonies and escapes as well . . .

1

SOHO SQUARE

Acting on a tip off from an informant, police raid a shady restaurant in Soho. The gangland villains have already got away, but have left behind them a menu with various doodles and words scribbled on it. Rumour has it that the gang are planning a new criminal operation. The police are keen to work out the codename of this venture.

Can the seemingly random jottings actually lead to revealing the codename of the operation?

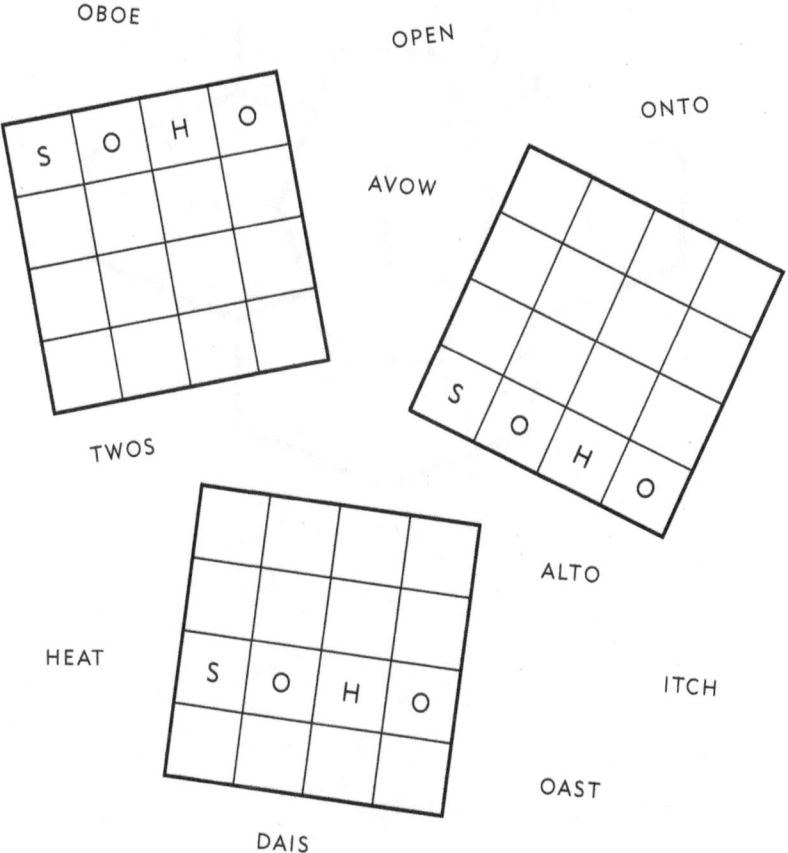

2

ILLUSION CUT DIAMOND

Hunting for stolen diamonds has featured in the work of Scotland Yard since its early days. An illusion cut diamond is one where the setting makes the stones look larger than they really are, i.e. things are not as they seem. In this puzzle things also are not straightforward. Fit the listed words back clockwise into the overlapping diamond shapes.

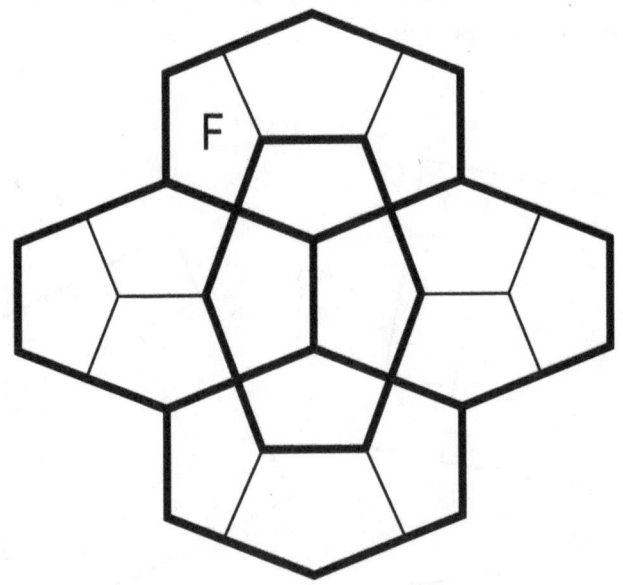

CALF

CHEF

EXIT

FIRM

FISH

3

THREE WAY SPLIT

Sometimes when you are on the run it is safer to split up than remain together. In this puzzle whole words have been split up and put in a random order. A word from the first column can join one from the middle column to make a word. Also each word from the middle column can join a word in the third column to make another word. Can you put them all back together again?

1 BANK	a) CUFF	i) BOOK
2 CROW	b) KICK	ii) FIELD
3 GOLD	c) BIRD	iii) TENDER
4 HAND	d) NOTE	iv) LINKS
5 JAIL	e) BAR	v) START
6 SIDE	f) MINE	vi) BATH

4

MISSING JEWELLERY

Beautiful (and valuable) jewellery has held a fascination for thieves from the notorious 'Harry the Valet' in the late nineteenth century to the Hatton Garden Heist in 2015.

Here we give you a list of items of jewellery and precious stones. Their names are hidden in the letter grid. Or are they? There is one item listed which is missing. Using all your powers of observation and attention to detail, can you compete with the most dogged of detectives and discover it? You are searching for something that isn't there!

A	E	M	E	C	R	A	L	D	I	A	T	M	O	S
T	R	M	M	B	R	O	O	C	H	E	E	P	D	L
C	U	A	E	M	E	Y	R	A	K	L	L	A	I	R
O	B	M	I	R	A	S	S	C	D	A	E	E	A	A
O	O	B	S	T	A	P	O	T	E	B	C	R	M	E
R	E	B	G	A	A	L	L	P	A	J	A	D	E	P
B	M	E	N	E	P	S	D	T	E	L	R	U	B	F
A	A	A	I	A	M	P	S	I	D	A	B	L	N	E
N	C	M	B	P	B	Y	H	R	A	T	R	I	R	W
G	H	B	R	O	H	B	T	I	E	M	A	L	A	T
L	A	E	A	T	B	U	I	N	R	H	O	T	S	O
E	A	R	E	E	A	R	R	G	C	E	C	N	O	P
N	I	M	E	J	N	A	A	S	R	H	C	P	T	A
C	A	O	B	O	G	G	N	I	R	R	A	E	I	Z
X	Y	N	O	E	L	C	E	C	A	L	K	C	E	N

AMBER	DIAMOND	ONYX
AMETHYST	EARRING	OPAL
BANGLE	EMERALD	PEARLS
BEADS	GARNET	RINGS
BRACELET	GEM	RUBY
BROOCH	JADE	SAPPHIRE
CAMEO	JET	TIARA
CHAIN	LOCKET	TOPAZ
CRYSTAL	NECKLACE	WATCH

5

MOVING THE MASTERPIECES

Priceless works of art by world famous painters are being moved around the city to different exhibitions. It is vital that word does not get out that these masterpieces are on the move so a cunning way of disguising the artists' names has been devised. Can you work it out? In each example the two artists have the same number of letters in their names.

1 D M E A G N E A S T

2 L O M O W R N E T Y

3 R S E T N U B O B I R S

4 T W A I R T H I A O L N

5 G A P U I C G A S U S I O N

6

THE INSPECTOR INVESTIGATES

Arthur Fiddler was found murdered one Sunday morning in his Mayfair penthouse. Arthur was well known to Scotland Yard, as were his five brothers who all earned a living by foul means rather than fair. When the Inspector began to delve deeply into the Fiddler family he found that Arthur was blackmailing each of his five brothers, who all were engaged in a different criminal activity, and who each paid him a regular amount of money on a different day of the week.

Using the information on the opposite page, can you work out the name of each Fiddler sibling, which criminal activity he specialised in, how much he paid to Arthur each week, and on which day the payment was made. Use the grid to help you, putting a tick when you find a piece of positive information and a cross when you can dismiss something. Cross refer until you have a full picture of the situation.

The fence, who paid Arthur on a Thursday, owed more than Charlie, who paid his £50 the day after the burglar made his payment.

Dick owed less than Frank and always paid on a Tuesday, which was before the forger's payment was made.

The conman owed twice as much as Eric, who paid on a Monday.

		BURGLAR	CONMAN	FENCE	FORGER	RACKETEER	MONDAY	TUESDAY	WEDNESDAY	THURSDAY	FRIDAY	£50	£500	£1,000	£3,000	£5,000
		CRIMINAL ACTIVITY					DAY PAID					AMOUNT PAID				
NAME	BOBBY															
	CHARLIE															
	DICK															
	ERIC															
	FRANK															
AMOUNT PAID	£50															
	£500															
	£1,000															
	£3,000															
	£5,000															
DAY PAID	MONDAY															
	TUESDAY															
	WEDNESDAY															
	THURSDAY															
	FRIDAY															

NAME	CRIMINAL ACTIVITY	DAY PAID	AMOUNT PAID

7

WITNESS STATEMENTS

A getaway van has sped away from the bank robbery. Six individuals make statements to the first police officer at the scene. Look at the vans below. All of them meet SOME of the criteria in the witness statements but only one van meets them all. Which van is it?

Witness 1 'The number plate was not straight.'
Witness 2 'It had a sticker in the passenger window.'
Witness 3 'The aerial was bent.'
Witness 4 'There were no windows at the side and at the back.'
Witness 5 'It wasn't a dark colour.'
Witness 6 'It wasn't a left hand drive.'

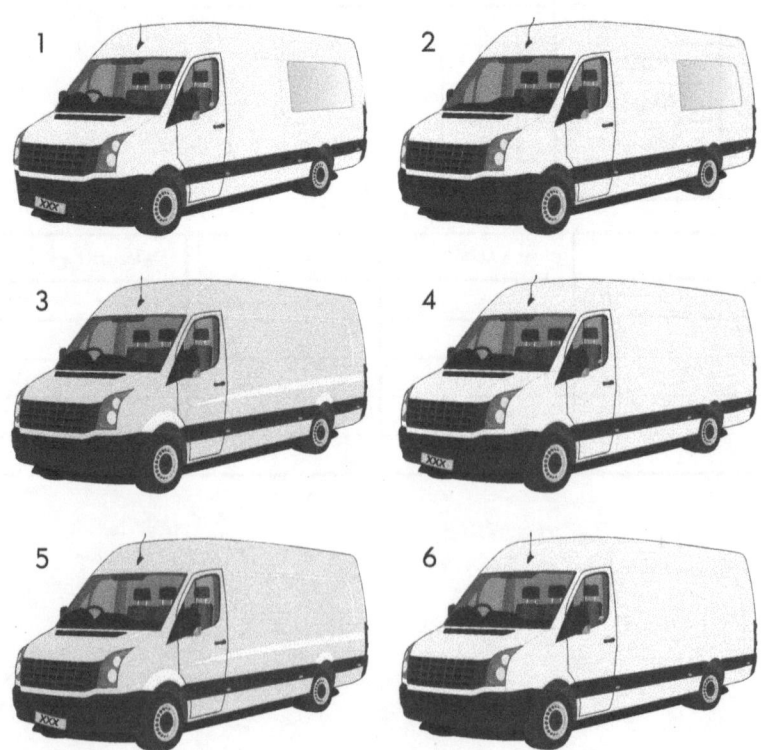

CHAPTER SEVEN

THE HINTERLAND OF HUMAN NATURE

In an age of brain scans – in which every flicker of emotion, every intellectual effort, can be analysed on a computer monitor – you would think that there would be no corner of the human psyche that could remain hidden. Yet, no computer can completely decrypt a criminal mind, so it remains up to detectives to continue to try to unravel the mysteries of the criminal psyche. This desire to understand evil goes right back to the days when Scotland Yard's detectives were working by pale gaslight, and when doctors were claiming that the shape of a man's skull with all its unique ridges and bumps was the key to determining his character.

For the detectives of Scotland Yard, the exercise of diving into a wrong-doer's mind is about long years of observation, examining the quirks of human nature, and its weaknesses and vulnerabilities. This experience in turn proves invaluable in anticipating the moves of repeat criminals. A constant alertness for deceit and inconsistency is key.

The puzzles in this section feature that sense of a mental duel. A need to be watchful so as to not have the wool pulled over your eyes, and also a sharpness for spotting the key details amid cunning misdirection. The great historical detectives of Scotland Yard, who in many cases rose to become household names, were each adept at the quicksilver reading of essential signs. From identifying scammers to brilliantly organised shoplifting gangs, the detectives were quick to imagine methods and means by which breathtaking crimes might be carried out. And this tightly focused imaginative skill was brought to bear on the more gothic crimes, too.

Perhaps the most famous of all Scotland Yard's detectives was Robert Fabian. Not least because when he retired and wrote his memoirs, they were deemed exciting enough to be turned into one of the very first hits of 1950s television. It was a show called *Fabian Of The Yard*. Fabian's methods were as far from Holmes as they could get. He believed in using the full panoply of Scotland Yard's resources, including its brilliant cross-referenced card file index. This index, filled with everything from convict information to unusual car registration plates, was the means of making quick links between apparently disparate clues before the age of computers.

'I soon realised,' said Fabian, 'that if I was going to beat the crook, I would have to study his methods and follow the reasonings of his warped mind.' And from the start of his career in the 1920s, he followed the advice given to him by an older officer: 'Give your eyes a chance.'

Eyes, and ears too. Early in his detecting career, Fabian was on the trail of another of those elegant jewel thieves who were such a feature of London rooftops in the interwar years. Like so many others, this particular character always opted for evening dress, and slipped in and out of apartments like a shadow. He was never seen and never heard.

Robert Fabian always had an avid appetite for the smallest clues, and one of these presented itself when a shoe-print was found in a flowerbed after an audacious heist. Something about the print pricked Fabian's curiosity more than usual. He had it analysed back at the Scotland Yard laboratory (like the cross-reference card index, this was a key weapon in the armoury for Fabian). The result confirmed his niggling suspicion; the shoe was a 'crepe rubber-soled evening dress shoe.' First, this was the sort of item, as he later noted, that 'no gentleman would wear'. Second of all, there were not that many shoe shops that stocked them.

Fabian and his associates visited each and every stockist, together with a copy of the print indicating the size and the style of the shoe. One shop in the West End recognised the shoe in question and was able to check the records to see which customer habitually favoured them. But the cunning thief was one silent step ahead: he had given a false name and address to the shoemaker.

The detective was unphased. He knew that this thief had a taste for Mayfair addresses and that his targets had all lived within quite a tight radius. So it was very likely that he would strike in that area again. Fabian's next move was every bit as cunning as his foe's. He spent a few evenings haunting the most fashionable Mayfair bars in the very swankiest hotels. His quarry dressed like a wealthy aristocrat, so there was every reason to believe that he would drink like one too. And Fabian's insight paid off brilliantly. One evening, as Fabian was positioned by the bar, a young man in full evening dress walked past him. The floor was parquet, and yet the young man passed him completely noiselessly.

Fabian discreetly followed the man through the London streets until finally, the man reached a house and walked in. The detective noted the address and shortly afterwards returned with a warrant. The man's home was found littered with sparkling jewels and an absurd amount of cash.

Another notable Fabian case was a warehouse heist that took place in the immediate post-war years. The sole clue was a tiny scrap of cloth torn from the jacket of one of the thieving heavies. This was once more a case for the Scotland Yard laboratory. The initial finding was dismaying. The cloth was from a demob suit of which, in the late 1940s, there were millions. These were suits issued to every man leaving the army and returning to civilian life. Nonetheless, the material had distinguishing features: chiefly, the pattern. Enquiries made to the Ministry of Supply established that the cloth was made near Somerset but was then sent to a Glasgow mill to be turned over for the mass production of suits.

Again, this was potentially disheartening, but visiting the Glasgow mill, Fabian learned from the supervisor the rule about stitching being individually identifiable, and from the fabric, he knew exactly who had worked on it. Stitching was 'like handwriting'. The man in question was called over and here was where Fabian's blend of patience and faith paid off. The worker remembered that he had been working on outsize suits and that this fabric was from a suit made for a man who was 6 foot 2 inches and also unusually broad.

Naturally, they had the man's address. Fabian and his colleagues, now travelling south to Birmingham, were able to arrest the warehouse thief and, in time, all of his associates. The criminal mind, Fabian knew, was obsessive about fine details and he had to be doubly so. Anything that might be overlooked or discounted by the transgressor could, with time and some skill, be turned against them. This was even true in the bizarre post-war case of the luxury hotel thief who across multiple heists, checked in as a guest, paid for the room, then ransacked all the other guests' rooms and departed. In all instances and under each different pseudonym, and with each different disguise, the thief left his own suitcase behind. And it was always weighted down with full beer bottles.

A quirky detail of no use to anyone, on the surface of it. Yet even here, Fabian saw his chance. All the bottles had had their labels carefully removed so they could not be identified. Except one, upon which a fragment of label remained with a fragment of a word: 'hoke'.

There was a pub not far away called 'The Artichoke'. Could this be where the burglar was buying his beer? After another bar stake-out and a sighting of a man buying an unusual quantity of bottled beer, the police found the man Fabian was seeking. This man (unnamed by Fabian in his memoirs) was something of an actor manqué. As well as containing a number of stolen items, the man's flat contained an unusual quantity of wigs and make-up. He had taken the disguises very seriously. The beer, however, was an element of genuine eccentricity; why on earth leave suitcases behind and why weigh them down in this singular manner? This psychological tic was useful to the police though; and if it had not been for Fabian's curiosity about the partially removed label, this otherwise crack thief might have got away with it.

Fabian was a brave man, too. In 1939, just before the outbreak of war, he was awarded the King's Medal for disarming an IRA bomb planted at Piccadilly Circus. One such device had already gone off but Fabian, with a pen-knife, had set about physically cutting the fuses on the other.

Some of Fabian's predecessors were also adept at out-thinking the malefactors. In the 1920s, Detective Fred 'Nutty' Sharpe (it is difficult to trace the source of this nickname) was on to a team of professional pickpockets who operated in and around the West End. Placing them under surveillance, he saw ten of them getting together to board a bus to take them to another district after a theft. As the gang moved to the upper deck, Sharpe swiftly boarded. Rather than having the bus brought to a halt, he moved to the cab window at the front and gave the bus driver some quiet instructions. Then he jumped off again and made for the nearest public telephone.

Passengers and pickpockets alike were puzzled when, first of all, the bus simply drove past a number of stops. Then, there was real bewilderment as the bus diverged from its route and started speeding down unfamiliar streets. It drew up outside a large police station. Outside were waiting a number of constables who had received the call from Sharpe. The thieves were arrested.

Another illustrious figure who used sharp intellect and a lively wit was Detective Frederick Wensley, who rose to be the head of the CID. He had started his career as something of an action man; to the delight of the popular press, he pursued a killer in Whitechapel up to the roof of a house, where, watched by a large crowd below, he physically fought the man and managed to subdue him. But following this he also developed a reputation as an incisive thinker. One newspaper described him as 'Sherlock Holmes in real life'. He was there at the forefront of the Siege of Sidney Street in 1911, when the police were forced to take on a band of armed eastern European revolutionaries who had robbed a bank and murdered several policemen. Elsewhere, he had the idea of infiltrating a notorious, and hugely profitable, gambling den by disguising himself as a soldier. At the pre-arranged time, he leapt from his chair and stood imperiously on top of a green baize table, calculating that the moment of bizarre shock would shield him from the more violent elements in the room as his fellow officers swept in.

And in 1917, when London was facing attacks from German zeppelins in the First World War, Wensley and his colleagues were faced with an unusual murder where the killer had left behind a particularly perplexing clue.

The victim was a woman called Emilienne Gerard, although it took a while to identify her. Various parts of her were found wrapped in a meat sack and a sheet in a sooty street near King's Cross station. An enigmatic note had been left behind with the body – it read 'Blodie Belgium!' Was this crime somehow prompted by the war? Was it in some way political? But the poor victim, who was French, had no affiliations or causes. And the method of disposing of her remains suggested that her killer was skilled in a very particular trade.

The first thread to follow was the sheet in which parts of her body had been wrapped. It had a laundry mark indicating the premises where it was regularly washed, and also indicating which customer it belonged to. From this, the Scotland Yard team was able to not only name the unfortunate victim, but also to find her address. They visited her flat and among the effects they found was the photograph of a Belgian butcher called Louis Voisin.

It appeared that Voisin and Emilienne had been in a relationship, but Wensley, when inviting Voisin to the station for questioning, knew that the butcher was hardly going to admit to anything more than that. Even though suspicions were strong, there was nothing even especially circumstantial that linked him to the strange and barbaric murder.

That was until Wensley had a moment of lightning bolt inspiration. Procuring paper and pen, he asked Voisin to write down the phrase 'Bloody Belgium!' Voisin did so, and Wensley asked if he could write it out a couple more times. It was noted that the handwriting style changed a little each time, probably in a conscious effort to disguise the natural style. But what was very much more striking was the spelling. Voisin had written out, three times, the phrase 'Blodie Belgium!' He genuinely thought this was how it was spelled, and thus did not bother to correct it. From here, Wensley proceeded to Voisin's Soho dwellings and in the cellar he found other parts of Emilienne Gerard. The crime, it was alleged, was essentially unpremeditated. Emilienne had paid an unexpected call on Voisin, her sweetheart, just as an air-raid had started. Entering his dwellings, she found that he was with another woman, Berte Roche. A desperate fight between her and Berte broke out and horribly, it appeared that Voisin then weighed in as well. His blows were so violent that Emilienne was killed on the spot.

What Voisin had then done, in trying to dispose of her so gruesomely, was an elaborate means of creating a false lead for police to follow. But Wensley, with his brilliant trap, secured the conviction. The butcher hanged; and the other woman, Berte, died while serving her prison sentence.

At that stage, psychology was an inexact science, and of course it still is. But as Freud's revolutionary theories about the subconscious spread deeper into society throughout the twentieth century, so the operatives of Scotland Yard and other police bureaux around the world began to turn with interest to doctors who specialised in the murkier corners of the human mind. One early criminal psychologist was Hans Gross, who averred that 'every thief has a characteristic style'. He studied a range of crimes and found that serial offenders had certain trademark characteristics.

In late 1920s Germany, a little before the economic firestorm of the Depression pitched the country into political darkness, there was an extraordinary and macabre case that saw the local police turn to a psychologist for help. A series of killings and attacks were being carried out by a figure dubbed 'The Dusseldorf Vampire'. Dr Ernst Gehnert was consulted and his considered ideas about the type of man who might be capable of such crimes was then treated as the psychological equivalent of a photo-fit. The reality, though, was that these ideas were rather one-dimensional. Dr Gehnert averred that the killer must have had a plausibly friendly manner to get so close to his victims before the attacks, and he was 'exceptionally cruel' and 'must be mad'. The killer, Peter Kürten, was eventually turned over to the police by his wife so Dr Gehnert's theories played no actual part in bringing him to justice. Nonetheless, this was among the very first instances of psychological profiling.

And as the years went on, Scotland Yard became increasingly interested in the idea of building up a sense of an offender's personality. They started to use experts who could pick their way through a maze of different manias and conditions. Practitioners such as Dr Patrick Tooley and Professor David Canter have helped Scotland Yard with investigations by pinpointing telltale characteristics that even the smoothest of sociopaths could not entirely disguise. And of course, the dream remains to identify such dangerous individuals before they ever have the chance to harm anyone else, a means of looking into the future of potentially criminal souls.

So the following puzzles, some in the form of logic problems, carry the extra implicit challenge that is presented on a daily basis to detectives: can you pick out likely suspects through certain personality quirks and oddities and certain sets of facts about whereabouts and habits?

1

DISCARD PILE

Four rows, four columns. Five sets of instructions. Follow the instructions and discard the irrelevant information to get to the truth and reveal the hidden message.

	1	2	3	4
A	NUT	WINGS	OWN	LIE
B	LET	SHY	CRY	BUY
C	SEA	APRON	DOGS	ARE
D	STEERING	SLEEPING	INTEGERS	ENERGIST

Discard every word which rhymes with another in row B.

Discard every word which sounds like a letter of the alphabet in row C.

Discard every word made solely of letters in the second half of the alphabet in row A.

Discard every theatre term in column 2.

Discard every word which is anagram of another in row D.

What is the message?

2

JUST THE OPPOSITE

Can you believe what you are told? How many times has a detective been sidetracked into thinking exactly the opposite of what he or she should have thought? Fortunately the correct solution usually comes to light in the end. In this puzzle you are given a clue, but the answer word that goes in the grid is its exact opposite.

ACROSS

8 Generosity (7)
9 Underweight (5)
10 Thin (5)
11 Early (7)
12 Tiny (4)
13 Calm (8)
16 Few (8)
18 Imprisoned (4)
21 Sly (7)
23 Keep (5)
25 Frailty (5)
26 Freeze (7)

DOWN

1 Fiction (4)
2 Cowardice (6)
3 Safe (5)
4 Villain (4)
5 Fraud (7)
6 Recipient (6)
7 Promote (8)
12 Ugly (8)
14 Me (3)
15 Kindness (7)
17 Bungle (6)
19 Madness (6)
20 Floppy (5)
22 Begins (4)
24 Misses (4)

3

THE WHOLE TRUTH

Dr Porkies runs a home for people who always tell lies. None of the people in his care ever make a statement that is true. Four residents – Charlotte, Donald, Simon and Vanessa – have spent the afternoon in different areas of the doctor's large house. One person was in the garage, one was in the greenhouse, one in the kitchen and one in the study. Dr Porkies asks the four people where they have been. One says, 'Donald was in the greenhouse.' The second speaker says, 'Donald, Charlotte and Vanessa were in the garage.' The third says, 'I was in the kitchen but I am not called Charlotte.' A fourth chips in to announce that, 'Donald was in the kitchen.'

From the statements made, Dr Porkies can place where everyone has been. Can you?

4

CHANCE IT

'It's very simple, Inspector,' smiled Charles Dancer. 'You want information but why should I give you any . . . That is assuming that I had any information to give. Perhaps if you chanced your arm at my little challenge I may possibly recall a fact or two for you.'

The Inspector and Charles Dancer – known as Chancer – were old adversaries. Charles loved a bet and any game of chance. He enjoyed cards and the casino wheel, but his greatest passion was for the less glamorous game of dominoes.

'There are two dominoes in place on a pattern set out on the table. Here are six more dominoes. Put them back to complete the pattern so that all four rows across, all four columns down and both diagonals have a total of 14,' said Dancer. 'Complete the challenge in three minutes and my memory may start flooding back.'

The Inspector completed the challenge. How did you get on?

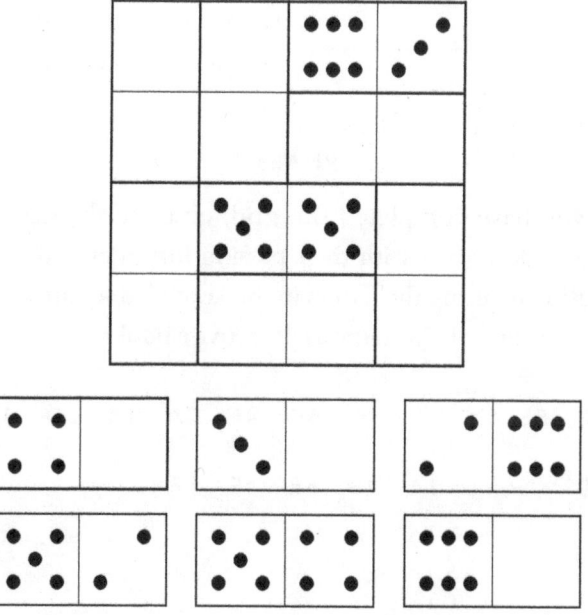

5

LAW AND ORDER

PHASE 1

Observing, sifting, cataloguing and checking information played a significant part in police work. Insert the missing words in the story below and slot your answers vertically in their correct places in the upper grid. The third row reading across will spell out the name of a famous Scotland Yard detective.

	1	2	3	4	5	6
A						
B						
C						
D						
E						
F						

'It was a glorious sunny (4) after-noon at the end of the week, and many people were enjoying a game of lawn (6) in the park. The London park was close to the river (2). A cup of (1) was poured from a thermos flask, and photographs were taken to fill the family (3) at a later date. A jolly gent (5) with laughter at someone's else's joke, and then there was a scream . . .'

PHASE 2

When you have completed the grid, emulate the dedication of those early detectives with their passion for order and cataloguing information by using the letters in the keycoded squares to spell out the name of one of this famous detective's books.

6A 2B 5E   3A 6D 4E 2A 1B 2D 4F

5B 1D   1A 4B 6E 3E 1F.

6

INFORMERS

Every good copper needs to have information from the streets. But how accurate were some of the reports from the coppers' narks? In a shady London pub, the Inspector has asked three trusted informers to watch the TWELVE members of a criminal gang. We can identify the gang members by the letters A to L. The Inspector needs to know in which order the individuals left the pub. Let's call the three informants X, Y and Z to keep their identities safe. They all report back, but their information does not match. The only individual who was incorrectly placed by all three informants was C. Every other person was correctly identified by at least one informer. Each informant got seven pieces of information incorrect. Informer Z thought that B was the eighth to leave but he was wrong!

The Inspector was watching the door from outside so he knows the order in which people left.

Can you work out the true order from the information on offer?

	1	2	3	4	5	6	7	8	9	10	11	12
X SAYS	C	I	B	F	A	J	E	K	D	H	L	G
Y SAYS	A	D	E	K	B	I	H	J	F	C	L	G
Z SAYS	H	C	E	D	G	L	J	B	F	A	K	I

7

FORGERY

Look at the six signatures. Five of them are forgeries. They may appear to be very similar, but only one matches every detail of the signature shown at the top of the page.

Can you spot the fakes?

Bertram Cripps

1 *Bertram Cripps*

2 *Bertram Cripps*

3 *Bertram Cripps*

4 *Bertram Cripps*

5 *Bertram Cripps*

6 *Bertram Cripps*

CHAPTER EIGHT

WATCHING THE DETECTIVES

In Britain and America, there are entire television channels devoted to police procedurals and whodunnits, and in bookshops across the world, fictional detective stories are snapped up in their millions. For many of the real-life detectives of Scotland Yard, these colourful yarns will have been a source of childhood fascination. How many would-be recruits were inspired by these fictional yet exciting depictions of bravery and ingenuity? Which heroic fictional detectives have become role models? And what happens when the border between fiction and reality is blurred?

The puzzles in this section reflect that occasionally curious crossover between truth and fiction, where real-life cases inspire films and novels, and where fiction inspires the real-life detectives of Scotland Yard; in particular, an intriguing selection of Locked Room mysteries drawn from vintage (and sometimes long-forgotten) detective novels.

In terms of giving shape to the reading public's idea of what a detective should be like, author Edgar Allen Poe led the way with his French sleuth August Dupin, who solved 'The Murders in the Rue Morgue' and the affair of 'The Purloined Letter' in the 1840s. Dupin was detached and very slightly otherworldly; traits that would later appear in many other fictional detectives.

There was an even more rounded fictional figure, several years later, the inspiration for whom was very firmly rooted in reality. Inspector Bucket, who moves through the pages of Charles Dickens's 1852 novel *Bleak House*, is engaging yet enigmatic, benign yet ever-watchful, electrically intelligent and yet tirelessly patient when his investigations take a wrong turn. *Bleak House* itself cannot be described as a whodunnit. The story of never-ending legal conflict and families with long-buried secrets goes far beyond that. But in it, Inspector Bucket investigates the murder of a character called Tulkinghorn. And his progress through this foggy, murky investigation takes him from the refined drawing rooms of titled aristocrats to the reeking slum of Tom-All-Alone's. Bucket is 'a sharp-eyed man in black', middle-aged, and with a noticeably prominent and plump forefinger, which he waves around in the air for emphasis at crucial moments in the story.

Bucket is a character who is able to move between all strata of society but there is something uncanny about his ubiquity. Sometimes he appears in rooms without any of the other characters being aware of him. He looks at people with an unnerving closeness and steadiness. And he specialises in wrong-footing those he is interested in, on one occasion attending a cheerful birthday party and giving a rendition of a hearty song, before changing his tune and arresting one of the guests. Inspector Bucket also uses one of the best-loved set-pieces of the fictional detective – seeming to have no more questions to ask the grand Sir Leicester Dedlock, he thanks him for his time, making to leave the room – only to turn at the door with one more piercing enquiry. This is a seemingly offhand observation about a reward poster that then leads to the Inspector pursuing a fresh possibility and a fruitful conversation with a footman bringing him closer to the truth.

One of fiction's first detectives, Bucket illustrated the philosophical possibilities of the role: whether lurking unobtrusively in the background, or leaping forward and taking the lead with gusto, he is always there to interpret an entire world, including its grim mysteries. He is there to see the threads that bind an interminable Court of Chancery case to long-buried family secrets. He is there to define what is deceitful and what is true. Charles Dickens was thought to have based Inspector Bucket upon Charles Frederick Field, a real Scotland Yard detective whose previously mentioned career proved a source of unending fascination. Bucket is also imbued with a sharp wit deployed against social superiors; and it is tempting to think that Dickens's admiration of Field extended to this element of detective work. That is, the man of humble origins not only moving through the salons of elegant society, but also – by virtue of his authority – commanding its attention and, indeed, obedience. Certainly in the decades to follow the archetype of the slightly eccentric, anti-establishment detective – from Father Brown to Columbo – would prove very popular.

Bucket is a figure who can plunge into impenetrable physical and metaphorical fogs and find his way through to the truth, guiding others along the way. Another rightly famed Victorian fictional detective is Wilkie Collins's Sergeant Cuff, who pursues the thief of an exquisite stolen diamond in *The Moonstone*, published in 1868. Here was another crossover from reality to fiction as Cuff was thought to be based on Scotland Yard's very own (and previously mentioned) Inspector Whicher.

Despite nineteenth-century crime fiction being regularly inspired by real life, it leapt far ahead of reality when it came to gender equality. Andrew Forrester's volume *The Female Detective* was published in 1864 and across seven short mysteries, a lady known to all only as 'G' (although her name is revealed as Miss Gladden) is assigned to cases by a baffled Scotland Yard. This was fifty years before women were even allowed to work in Voluntary Women's Patrols at the Yard. Even more sensational was the arrival a few months later of Mrs Paschal, a widow lending her services to the Yard, in *Revelations of a Lady Detective* written by William Stephens Hayward.

Mrs Paschal was a dynamic figure. She immersed herself in gothic mysteries involving nuns, investigated countesses with suspicious wealth, and risked her own life to infiltrate secret societies. Mrs Paschal's ability to draw the reader into exciting situations of jeopardy, and to thrill with cases that were both colourful and baroque, must surely have put down markers for many fictional detectives to come.

By the twentieth century, detective fiction was so ubiquitous that real-life cases were being presented by newspapers in the sensationalist style of fiction, accompanied by action-packed graphics. Heists aimed at jewellery shops and banks were illustrated with artistic representations of black cars driving off at speed, and in the immediate post-war years there were even some (rare) London shoot-outs that when depicted in black and white artwork gave the city a flavour of downtown Chicago. Robert Fabian had a regular newspaper slot which was often illustrated with dramatic line drawings of hoodlums diving into getaway vans or of the grim faces of killers peering out from behind bars.

While real life was treated as melodrama, some fictional police stories became markedly more realistic. In the 1950s, novelist John Creasey wrote a number of novels centring on Scotland Yard's Commander George Gideon. This figure, looming of frame, soft of voice, was faced with an array of different crimes; everything from sinister murders to racehorse fixing to runaway children to a band of intellectual nihilist thugs. Creasey also gave Gideon a family life, something rarely, if ever, seen in police dramas. Since Gideon was a determinedly hands-on officer, there was always the sharp tension between moments of sweaty jeopardy – with shotgun-wielding gang members or a tormented scientist with a homemade bomb – and the glimpses of Gideon's domestic life. His wife was patient but sometimes anxious, and the smaller of his children were perennially fascinated by the cases he solved. Gideon's strength was his understanding of human nature built up over many decades on the job. He had the ability to judge who was truly dangerous, and who might be rehabilitated. Scotland Yard as an institution was also portrayed as having an aim – through its meticulously kept records, its array of experts and its patrols of decent young constables – of a benevolent omniscience. The Yard would protect the innocent, wherever they were, from the predations of wrong-doers. George Gideon was tough but realistic, a great source of inspiration for future Yard detectives.

At the other end of the spectrum is poor Inspector Lestrade, a 'sallow-faced' man doomed to remain a hundred steps behind fiction's greatest detective, Sherlock Holmes. And, of course, the eternal popularity of the Sherlock Holmes stories means that this most unflattering depiction of Scotland Yard is endlessly reiterated. Thankfully, though, Lestrade's character was handsomely rehabilitated in a recent modern-day television adaptation. As imagined by Steven Moffatt, Lestrade (played by Rupert Graves) is no longer a hapless character, but a decent public servant who stands up for Holmes when others find his selfish genius too much to take. This Scotland Yard operative is taken for a fool but is actually an active participant in some of Sherlock's more baroque adventures; always exasperated but clever enough to see that Holmes's preternatural gifts repay the faith Lestrade has in him.

At the more serious, thoughtful end of the crime genre is an enduring figure created by P. D. James. Adam Dalgliesh, who stands as the best advertisement in fiction for Scotland Yard, is the detective who features in fourteen of her novels. Dalgliesh not only writes poetry, he has had his poetry published. Intelligence and sensitivity combine to brilliant effect in his character. Indeed, P. D. James said straightforwardly of her creation that 'I simply produced the kind of hero I'd like to read about; courageous but not foolhardy, compassionate but not sentimental.' And there is every chance that P. D. James's approach to the entire business of detective stories helped act as a recruitment sergeant for the real Scotland Yard. Whodunnits from earlier years tended to be more focused on the puzzle of the murder, rather than the characters, whereas James was aiming for more psychological realism. 'From the start, I felt that what I was doing was examining human beings under the strain of an investigation for murder,' she told the *Guardian* in 2011. 'And such an investigation tears down all the walls of privacy that we build around ourselves and reveals us for who we are.'

Understanding the darker corners of human nature without letting the knowledge sour their general view of humanity is the idealised virtue of fictional detectives but their real-life counterparts were always under pressure to exhibit these same qualities themselves. And often, qualities of fictional detectives are impossible to replicate in reality. Scotland Yard detectives in real life must face the gruesome, the horrible and the fearful every day, without the benefit of plot devices and rewrites.

The current popularity of detective fiction, in print and on television, suggests that the public is always eager to hear more of the stresses, as well as the triumphs, of crime-fighting. We all like to imagine that – like Hercule Poirot or Harriet Vane and Peter Wimsy – amateurs like ourselves can navigate the complex labyrinths of murder investigations. The puzzles here are directly about the challenge that authors have thrown open to their millions of readers: the delightful game of collusion that has come to be known as the Locked Room mystery.

THE FINEST LOCKED ROOM MYSTERIES

Here are puzzles that real-life Scotland Yard detectives would have relished tackling in their spare time over the years. Fictional murder has often walked along the borders of the fantastical and so many mysteries have been tinged with suggestions of the uncanny and the supernatural. But perhaps what these conundrums have in common with real life is that the detectives are there to ground us with empirical evidence.

The Locked Room mystery is a category of detective story that has intrigued and inspired writers from Sir Arthur Conan Doyle to Agatha Christie. These seemingly impossible riddles where corpses are found in rooms locked from the inside come in the most astonishing variety and are ceaselessly ingenious. But the very conscious game being played with readers is also a reminder of what real-life detectives do: they look at the fragments of a problem, the disparate elements that are not immediately obvious, and from these strands of inchoate information they assemble a world in which rationality is restored.

There is philosophy here: no problem is insoluble. So the puzzles in this section are ten of the finest vintage locked room mysteries. A note: the answers at the back will naturally contain spoilers, so those who do not wish to know the solution to some of the stories here might prefer to get a hold of the books themselves!

1

MURDERS IN THE RUE MORGUE
by Edgar Allen Poe

It is reasonable to claim that the mid nineteenth century American master of the macabre popularised the hugely enjoyable Locked Room murder mystery genre. In this short story from 1841, the scenario is as follows . . .

A mother and daughter have been gruesomely murdered at their apartment, several storeys up, in the Rue Morgue, Paris. The mother's body – almost decapitated – has been taken from the apartment and is found in the back yard of the building. Meanwhile, her daughter is discovered strangled, and weirdly stuffed up inside the apartment chimney. The room in which these murders occurred was – naturally – still locked from the inside. The clues, as examined by the detective Dupin, are these: a bag of gold coins; several tufts of grey hair; a bloodied razor blade; and curious conversations overheard by neighbours, seemingly from within the room, at around the time of the murders. The conversations seemed to be two men talking; one in French, the other in a wholly unknown language. What could have prompted such crazed murders? Why these two women? Who were the talking men, and what did their discussion portend?

2

THE ADVENTURE OF THE SPECKLED BAND
by Sir Arthur Conan Doyle

The creator of Sherlock Holmes delighted in adding layers of intricacy and sharp-eyed detail to the genre: rooting the fantastical and the bizarre in realistically depicted Victorian London streets, suburban villas and Home Counties country houses. Here was one of his most fondly received head-scratchers . . .

Helen Stoner is in fear for her life; and more particularly, she is frightened by her stepfather Dr Roylott. Since the death of her mother, and her twin sister, Helen has been living with Dr Roylott at a smart mansion in Surrey; she engages Holmes and tells him of the sinister circumstances of her twin sister's death. The sister died two weeks before she was to be married, and her last desperate words to Helen were: 'The Speckled Band!'

Dr Roylott is having the large house renovated; and this necessitates Helen Stoner having to move into the room once occupied by her late sister. Holmes and Watson inspect it and make various curious discoveries: the cord used for summoning servants does not work; the bed is fixed firmly to the floor; and there is a ventilator hole that passes from this room through to the bedchamber of Dr Roylott. No matter how securely locked this room will be, nothing, it seems, can stop death entering . . . but how?

3

THE CASE OF THE CONSTANT SUICIDES
by John Dickson Carr

A castle in the Highlands of Scotland, a tower and a life insurance policy that will not pay out if the insured party has killed himself. John Dickson Carr specialised in Locked Room mysteries and this is considered by many to be one of his most entertaining, with flashes of black comedy peppering the sinister mystery. The room this time is the bedroom at the top of the tower in the Castle of Shira. It can only be reached by means of a spiral staircase. There are no secret passages. Alex Campbell is the insured party whose body is found at the rocky base of that tower; and if the tragedy is proven to be suicide, there will be no money for the beneficiaries of his will. But if he was pushed out of the window, from a room with a locked door, how did the murderer do it? A collapsible wire animal cage is found under the bed; and there is also a suggestion that the ghost of a mutilated Highlander roams abroad. On top of this, another character decides to spend the night in the room to see if there is something preternatural going on and is in turn found next morning at the base of the tower, severely injured. Once again, the window was open and the door was locked from the inside . . . The key to the mystery lies in atmosphere – in more ways than one!

4

THE BIG BOW MYSTERY
by Israel Zangwill

Published in 1892 – and serialised daily in one of the more lurid newspapers – this was one of the first full length Locked Room murder mysteries. Set in London's East End, just several years after the Ripper murders, it is packed with juicy social detail as well as some fine dark humour. And because of its episodic nature, readers wrote in with ingenious theories even as the tale was unfolding . . .

A young man – Arthur Constant – lives in a boarding house run by Mrs Drabdump. One morning, she cannot wake him, and his door is locked, with the key still in the lock on the inside; she has a premonition of the worst and calls for the aid of a neighbouring retired detective. Together they force the door, and the detective advises the landlady to look away from the horror.

The young man is in his bed – but as Mrs Drabdump, after a few moments, peers fearfully, she sees that his throat has been cut from ear to ear. The windows are secure; and there is no sign of a murder weapon anywhere in the room. As news spreads, so too do the theories, including that of suicide. But if that is the case, then there should be a bloodied blade. Such an item is conspicuous by its absence.

This is a case that comes to encompass suspects galore, and walk-on parts from dockworkers to William Gladstone. Who could have hated this apparently blameless young man so much? But more: how the Dickens did the killer get in; and where then did the fatal blade go? The key to the mystery is time.

5

THE MYSTERY OF THE YELLOW ROOM
by Gaston Leroux

From the author of *Phantom of the Opera* came a classic Locked Room mystery in 1907 that was admired by Agatha Christie among others. A grand chateau; a scientist working on theories of 'the dissociation of matter', making solid objects disappear; his daughter, whose bedchamber, the 'Yellow Room', is adjacent to his laboratory; and that daughter being heard to scream, and then being found close to death, with the door locked on the inside and the window securely barred.

How could the putative assassin have escaped – and with such speed? As the mystery deepens, the detective and his rival investigator, a journalist, are at the Chateau as further attacks happen, but they appear to be faced with a vanishing assassin, who can disappear into thin air at any sign of pursuit.

Leroux provided diagrams and maps of the Chateau for his readers; could the would-be killer really be linked to the 'dissociation of matter' itself? But the key to the mystery is more to do with perception than matter itself . . .

6

THE ABSENCE OF MR GLASS
by G.K. Chesterton

A lighter-hearted Locked Room conundrum, set in Yorkshire, which pits the clerical detective Father Brown against a baroque assailant. The set-up: young James Todhunter is romancing Maggie McNab. They are to be married; but there is a secret that Todhunter – who lives in an upstairs room in a boarding house – is keeping from his love. He frequently keeps his bedroom door firmly locked. On previous nights, Todhunter has been heard through the door of his room having angry words with a mystery visitor called Mr Glass. No one has ever seen this gentleman entering or leaving but Maggie, listening intently through the door, has previously heard Todhunter utter this man's name.

Now Maggie calls for the priest in a panic because she has heard sounds of violence within the room. They break down the door and find Todhunter alive but tied up in a corner. There is no one with him, but the priest sees a discarded top hat and several smashed tumblers of whiskey.

Who then is the sinister Mr Glass and how has he vanished into thin air? In this conundrum, the shattered tumblers are key.

7

SO LONG AT THE FAIR

by Anthony Thorne

A twist to the genre: a baffling mystery set in Paris, 1889, at the time of the city's Great Exhibition. Vicky has travelled to France from England with her brother Johnny; they book into their hotel, and despite the fact that her brother is tired, Vicky insists they go to see Montmartre.

Upon returning to the hotel, Vicky goes up to her room, leaving her brother downstairs having a final nightcap. Whilst drinking, Johnny gets into a conversation with two other English guests.

In the morning, Vicky rises, goes to her brother's room, but rather than being locked, the room is no longer there!

Where the door was, there is simply blank wall. Bewildered, Vicky goes to reception and the staff are mystified by her mention of a room number that isn't used. Not only that, they absolutely deny having booked her brother in the previous evening. She cannot find anyone to confirm that her brother even existed.

No one has ever seen this 'Johnny'; and the room is a room that never was. But the key to this sinister puzzle lies in Johnny's tiredness that previous evening . . .

8

THE MIRACLE OF MOON CRESCENT
by G.K. Chesterton

Another classic head-scratcher for Father Brown, this time in America, where he faces not just a locked room but a mysteriously transported corpse. Warren Wynd is the millionaire victim in question. And the set-up involves the priest and several others waiting outside the man's office one evening on the second floor of his premises in Moon Crescent, a curving terrace.

The mystery begins with a sharp bang from outside: someone down below at the back of the building has fired some kind of shot.

And after those initial moments of confusion, there is the realisation that Wynd has been locked away in his office for longer than expected. The door is duly broken in – but the millionaire has vanished.

It is only when Father Brown and his acquaintances are later walking around the grounds of Moon Crescent in the darkness when they see a tree with what appears to be a broken branch. But it is no branch: it is in fact the hanging body of the millionaire, with a noose around his neck. But what on earth happened between him sitting in a locked room at his desk, and ending up in those branches? The key to this murder mystery lies in the perils of looking down . . .

9

THE NAME OF THE ROSE
by Umberto Eco

A spectacular literary tribute to the art of both detection and detectives is this richly atmospheric thriller set in a medieval monastery in Italy in the twelfth century. Here, a Franciscan monk from England, Brother William of Baskerville, has been called in by the Abbott to solve the mystery of a young scribe found dead; and almost as soon as he arrives, the bodies begin piling up around the monastery, and the murders seem to have an apocalyptic theme. Do they really signify that the End of Days is approaching?

There is also a Locked Room mystery: the monastery has an ancient library, a vast tower on the edge of a sheer cliff. This library has been constructed as a treacherous labyrinth to frighten away the uninitiated. Deep within is a room with no apparent door, but a window facing out over the sheer cliff. Where there should be a door to this room is instead a mirror that shows frightening illusions of phantoms.

However, for anyone who does somehow find their way in, this locked room contains a book that kills. Anyone perusing its forbidden contents are, like cursed people, doomed to die violently soon afterwards.

The word 'Quatuor' written over the non-existent door comes with a clue from one such dying victim who found a way in: 'The hand over the idol works on the first and seventh of the four'. . . In this locked room, how can a simple book bring death upon those who read it?

10

CRIME IN NOBODY'S ROOM

by John Dickson Carr

A block of flats in Chelsea, London, 1938; a young tenant, Ronald Denham, back from a boozy night out, goes up to his floor. In his drunkenness, he opens the door, walks in to the flat, and it takes him a moment to woozily wonder if he has somehow got the wrong apartment.

The furnishings are different from his own – oriental lampshades, a large painting in sepia – plus there is also the murdered body of an old man sitting in a chair. For some reason, the corpse is wearing a beige raincoat inside out so that the coat's green lining is on the outside.

Denham is then knocked out with a cosh . . . And when he comes to in the communal corridor outside that floor of apartments, his neighbours are perplexed. The flat he described does not exist!

But the corpse that he described does. The old man's stabbed body is subsequently found in the lift. He was a property developer, and known to several of the neighbours . . .

Colonel March of Scotland Yard's 'Department of Queer Complaints' is on the case. How to explain the flat that isn't there? And who among the tenants committed this most ingenious crime? The key to it all, the Colonel realises, is that the killer is colour blind . . .

CHAPTER NINE

FOOTSTEPS IN THE FOG

In the Scotland Yard archive, colourful maps that could be mistaken for works of art show Victorian London divided into an array of different segments, each with a large letter superimposed. These maps show each segment shaded either red, blue, yellow or orange – not to signify crime levels, but simply to render each district clear and distinct. They show how Scotland Yard organised the policing of London throughout the late nineteenth century. From the elegant hub of Piccadilly Circus to the clamour of the docks, each division was assigned a letter of the alphabet, with 'A' signalling Westminster and the area of the Yard itself. Constables and stations worked and patrolled these patches and got to know them intimately.

The story of Scotland Yard through the years has helped paint a picture of the social tides of the city, and of its changing landscapes; not just the ubiquitous fogs, through which constables walk and screams echo, but also the less salubrious quarters which would most likely have been left out of any glossy guidebooks. The winding alleys and dangerous areas had to be charted, catalogued, and carefully monitored by the Yard, and, more often than not, this intimate knowledge of each and every shadow on London's streets was hugely valuable. Chasing criminals is a lot easier when you know the shortcuts . . .

The puzzles in this section are therefore based around London's geography. There are games involving tempting historical targets, labyrinthine escape routes, criminal landmarks in Soho and down at the docks, with some even inspired by the Tower of London (since surely every self-respecting super-criminal has at one point or another turned his thoughts to the mouth-watering prospect of the Crown Jewels, even if they would be a little tricky to sell on afterwards). The best detectives can negotiate these mazes effortlessly, but can you?

In the earliest days of the police, before London had ballooned outward into a vast metropolis, some of the city's central districts had an extraordinarily tough and squalid character. St Giles was among the most notorious; with hideous over-crowding, people stupefying themselves with gin and every sort of crime a daily occurrence. St Giles is now the area that lies between New Oxford Street and Charing Cross Road and is full of luxury flats, swanky offices and trendy bars. Also best avoided in the nineteenth century was Saffron Hill; a district of closely-built slum housing on the banks of the reeking River Fleet. It was around here that Charles Dickens's Fagin operated with his gang of child thieves. Today there are tech start-ups and hipster coffee joints.

Despite their squalor, these and other Victorian districts acquired an air of gothic romance. Long before the hideous Jack the Ripper murders of 1888, Whitechapel, Stepney and other neighbourhoods in the East End of London had become a subject of some fascination thanks to the 'Police Intelligence' reports that featured in most newspapers. These locations proffered plenty of content, from violence to riots, even as far as body-snatching from the churchyard in Poplar.

The areas closest to the docks – which in the Victorian era fell within 'F' Division – needed sensitive policing at all times. In the earliest days of the force, Sir Robert Peel gave careful thought to the best kind of recruits for his new service, and there was a great effort made to employ constables of Irish heritage. The reason, very simply, was that the streets around Shadwell and Ratcliffe were filled with a great many Irish families who had moved to London looking for work. They resided in a landscape full of warehouses, great sailing ships, railways and factories, which provided plenty of dark corners for harbouring crime. Peel hoped that Irish residents would feel more at ease with police who might have some understanding of their circumstances, but it did not always quite work out in this way and some of these constables found themselves at the receiving end of abuse. This came from both Irish families who felt that their uniformed countrymen were actually an oppressive tool of the state, and also from non-Irish offenders who complained that these officers were 'hot-headed'.

The docks were also a hotbed of intrigue and conflict for Scotland Yard because of the dazzling range of cultures that came to settle in the area. The German population of Shadwell, in particular its young drinking men, were partial to getting into battles with Irish neighbours, and come the turn of the century, prompted by the racist fictions of Sax Rohmer and his super-criminal/mastermind Dr Fu Manchu, there was a lurid fascination with the Chinese community in Limehouse. Many believed the district was riddled with opium dens. It was not. Nonetheless, the local police had to be assiduous in ensuring that gangs of whatever variety could not get a secure footing in the damp alleys and passageways that ran along the curve of the dark river.

Curiously, some London areas still carry subliminal associations with their lurid pasts. The exquisitely fashionable Hoxton, for instance, in its more crumbling, entropic corners, and little alleys of brick and cobbles, and occasional preserved shop-fronts, somehow continues to evoke a folk memory of the district's 1930s razor gangs, even amid all the exclusive nightclubs. Elsewhere, some addresses acquired such terrible notoriety that they had to be erased from the London map altogether. One such location was Rillington Place, in a run-down corner of north Kensington. The slayings that took place in this house in the late 1940s – truly hideous crimes committed by John Reginald Christie – led first of all to an innocent man, a lodger called Timothy Evans, being mistakenly convicted and hanged for the murder of his wife and baby daughter. But a few years later, in 1953, Christie moved out; and the new lodgers discovered corpses behind a hidden alcove in his kitchen, and the body of Christie's wife under the floorboards. The story was so nightmarish that the eventual slum clearance of the street allowed its name to be rubbed out. In its place there is now a peaceful mews backing on to the Hammersmith and City line.

Throughout the twentieth century, it was Soho that came to symbolise all that was transgressive about the capital. There were dens of vice, ruthless gangs, strippers, and a whole seething concourse of punters and mobsters. The tight streets and alleys acquired a whole new luminous life after dark, with scarlet lights luring excited customers through the doors of dubious establishments. There was a vicarious thrill here for the newspaper-reading public, especially when it was suggested that among the patrons of the seedier clubs were senior establishment figures including judges, MPs and peers. Alongside this was a certain transgressive comedy about the efforts of the police in trying to prosecute for obscenity.

One such case, in the 1960s, centred around a club owner called Quinn. His establishment featured a salty blend of striptease artistes and comedians telling extremely rude jokes. Surreptitious film had been taken of the acts on the stage. One young lady danced with a whip, which was occasionally cracked theatrically. Another removed her clothing while simultaneously handling several snakes which were being 'charmed' by the music. She then appeared to swallow one. There was an act involving a young lady called 'Bonnie Bell – The Ding Dong Girl'. She had bells on carefully-placed tassels that audience members were permitted to ring. This was altogether too much: a case was brought before the courts on the grounds that this was an 'unruly house'; the judge proclaimed it 'filthy, disgusting and beastly' (it is worth asking: how many other members of the legal profession were then among the thousands of furtive members of this club?). The young club owner was fined a then eye-watering £5000. The club owner's real name was Paul Raymond and it was not long before his particular brand of stage entertainment, Bonnie Bell and all, was accepted as a legitimate part of the Soho landscape.

This vista of pimps and gangs, strippers and club-owners, card sharps and illegal gambling premises put Soho at the heart of so many of Scotland Yard's departments. Up until the start of the 1960s, any young lady appearing completely nude on a stage was required by law to be completely still. To get around this performers would assemble 'tableaux' with titles such as 'Paris By Night' with women arranging themselves in the shape of the Arc de Triomphe and the Eiffel Tower. One evening, a party of drunken journalists watched the female performers troop on to the stage. As they started disrobing, one witty young hack shouted as a joke: 'Mother! How *could* you?' His fellow punters were not amused at having the spell broken and a fight began that soon assumed Wild West proportions. The police were quickly called to break it up.

There have been many other areas of London that have earned their place on the map thanks to their notorious criminal reputations, and one of these is Hatton Garden, near Holborn. For about 150 years, this otherwise drab thoroughfare has glittered with diamonds, exquisite precious stones, and stunning gold and silver jewellery. To protect this street of flashing beauty, merchants have always invested in the most up-to-date and innovative security, because of course Hatton Garden has provided the most irresistible temptation for generations of thieves. The most recent heist, an elaborate attack on a sealed vault in 2015, was both reprehensible and curiously quaint; the sort of crime one might see in a film from the 1950s.

It involved a quiet Bank Holiday; a lift shaft; an industrial drill; and thieves of a certain age. They managed to get away with an extraordinary sum, some twenty-four-million pounds' worth of rare stones and gold. But the methods that Scotland Yard employed to catch and convict them were rather more modern than the vintage villains had bargained for. Understanding that the audacious raid was carried out by experienced hands, the Metropolitan Police did not have to scour records for very long to see the echoes and patterns in previous heists. The twenty-first century twist saw the deployment of number-plate recognition software, and sophisticated hidden cameras. Some time after the raid, the suspects met up in a pub on the Pentonville Road and were filmed and recorded discussing the triumph of their theft. Here was the quintessential London crime, thwarted by a very modern Scotland Yard.

In an earlier age, another London landmark that hit the headlines was the Savoy Hotel, known across the globe for its elegance and luxury. In 1923, it hosted a wealthy young Egyptian, Ali Fahmy, who had bestowed upon himself the title 'Prince'. He was there with his wife Marguerite Alibert ('the Princess') and his manservant. They had one of the finest suites in the building, but from the very start of their visit, it seemed embarrassingly clear that this fashionable couple were in a state of almost perpetual acrimony. He was young; just 23 years old. She was ten years his senior. And it was noted everywhere they went that both of them seemed to be trying to cover up facial cuts and bruises. They did not seem able to disguise their mutual loathing.

One spring evening, on an unusually warm and humid night, the glamorous couple went to the theatre to see a production of *The Merry Widow* and they returned to the Savoy for a late supper. They caused consternation when the Princess threatened to hit her husband over the head with a wine bottle and he replied that if she did, he would do exactly the same back to her. With the meal over, she retired upstairs, and he went out into that uncomfortably warm night, seen hailing a cab in the direction of Piccadilly.

He was seen returning to the hotel at around 2 a.m.. By this time, the muggy night air was filled with hollow booms and sharp cracks; a wild thunderstorm had broken out along the Thames. As he approached his suite, Prince Ali Fahmy was seen by a hotel porter, who witnessed the Prince opening the door of his room, crouching and talking to his small dog. There were further terrific booms from the sky above, and as the porter walked away he thought he heard more defined cracks among them.

He made his way back along the corridor and there, through the open doorway, he saw Fahmy's wife standing over the Prince's bleeding body and saying repeatedly to herself (in French): 'What have I done, my dear?' The revolver with which she had shot him had been tossed aside on a sofa.

From the point of view of Scotland Yard, there was hardly any difficulty in detecting who had committed the crime, and Marguerite Alibert was swift to confess. But when it came to the matter of why she had done it, her subsequent trial for murder was sensationally turned upside down. The jury was told of her husband's 'unnatural' desires and demands and of his drastic use of servants to oppress and restrict her every move. The jury was told that he was a monster, and she was his prisoner and the defence argued that her actions could only be seen as self-defence. Extraordinarily, the jury acquitted her. Behind all of this was a series of deeply racist assumptions about the behaviour of the Egyptian prince. This case came to fruition at the height of other sensationalist reports concerning the white slave trade. But the broader point was that the Savoy, swankiest of all West End landmarks, acquired the same kind of notoriety as the more usual crime scenes.

Not that long ago, the Tower of London, home to the Crown Jewels and inspiration for countless heist daydreams, made the headlines when an intruder hit a streak of luck, having clambered over a wall late at night. The intruder was eventually detected by the Tower's cutting-edge security measures and picked up by the police but, having chanced upon an empty guard hut and some keys, he got a little further through the layers of security than even he might have been expecting. It was a rare and extraordinary breach. Thankfully, the Crown Jewels remained safe, as indeed they have been since 1671, when one Colonel Blood succeeded in reaching them. His was an exquisite and carefully calculated plan. Posing as a parson, Blood contrived to become friends with one of the wardens at the Tower. Weeks went by and their social ties deepened, with Blood's wife getting to know the warden's wife. After a suitable amount of time, Blood asked the warden if he might take a friend to see the Crown Jewels, then kept underground behind a metal grille. The warden was delighted to oblige his gentle friend the parson. And it was only when the parson's associate knocked him out that he understood he had been taken for a fool.

Blood and his associate started trying to pack as many of the jewels into their clothing as possible, but as they did so, Edwards the warden regained consciousness and started shouting about murder and treason. Blood was apprehended. This was a violent crime against the Crown, yet there were those who had nothing but admiration for Blood's guile. As we know, often such ambitious criminals tended to get admiration from the public who looked at such cases through rose-tinted glasses. Among those was King Charles II himself, who was fascinated when the miscreant was brought before him, and Blood was acquitted.

The one institute in London that seems to have always been secure from the attentions of predatory criminals is the Bank of England. Save the ingenious scheme cooked up by Alec Guinness and Stanley Holloway in *The Lavender Hill Mob* (1949) – stealing the bank's gold ingots, melting them down and turning them into souvenir models of the Eiffel Tower – the Old Lady of Threadneedle Street has always been too impenetrable a target. Of course, that particular district has its own bespoke City of London police.

As for the rest of the capital, famous locations of dastardly crime have become part of the rich tapestry of London's underworld history. Tourists come from all over the world to visit the streets of Whitechapel, the Tower of London and the Clink. There are some particular districts of the city that always seem to attract crime and criminals; equally, though, these streets have also inspired great crime-fighting. It is not just about knowing where gangs meet; it is about understanding the very fabric and history of those areas that seem to have been more prone to outbreaks of transgression than others. And from the East End to the leafy heights of Hampstead, the crimes that Scotland Yard face seem to have a certain degree of consistency. With the grand villas of north and south London attracting the light-fingered, and the back streets of Shoreditch playing host to drunkenness and narcotics (though in a rather trendier fashion now than in the late nineteenth century), patterns have been established across the decades. So the puzzles that follow pay tribute to that very specialised brand of local knowledge; the feel for the essential bones of the city that keep the Yard perennially one step ahead.

1

MIND YOUR MANORS

It always helps to know your own patch. Officers take pride in knowing the geography of their own 'manor'. Here is an aerial view of a suburban area.

Can you locate the position on the map of the square shown at the top of the page? There is one segment of map that exactly matches this square.

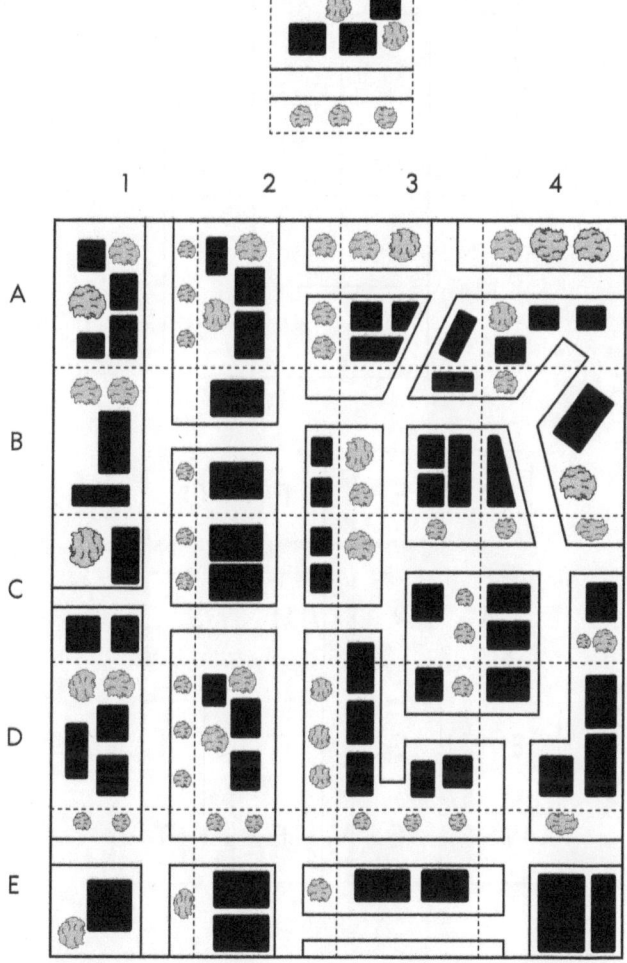

2

BLOCKS

Fit the blocks into the grid so that each horizontal and each vertical row spells out a word, i.e. five horizontal words and four vertical ones. Hopefully by the end you will have emerged from the fog.

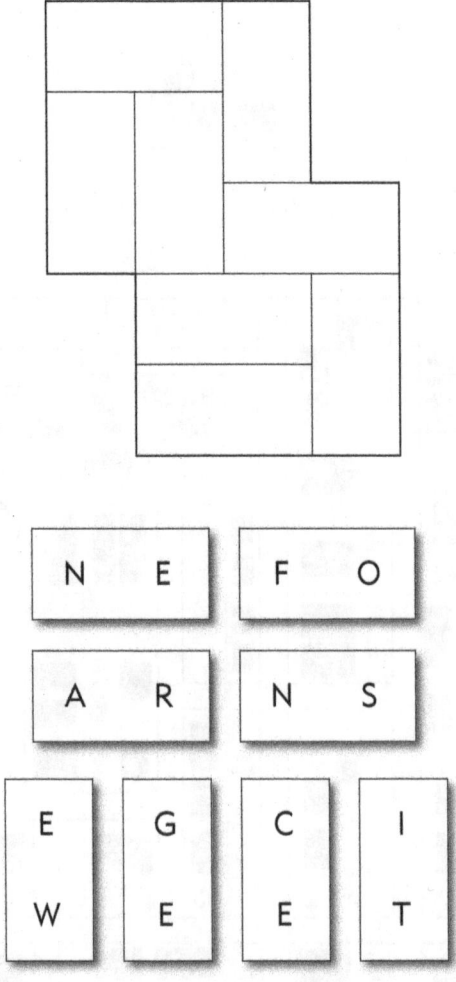

3

A STEP AT A TIME

The bobby on the beat knows to take a step at a time when out and about. There is a set starting point and a clear finishing point to be reached.

In this challenge, link the top word to the bottom one, changing a letter at a time and making new words at every step.

1   T   E   N   T   H

— — — — —

— — — — —

— — — — —

— — — — —

P   L   A   C   E

2   S   W   O   R   D

— — — — —

— — — — —

— — — — —

— — — — —

C   H   A   S   E

4

NO HIDING PLACE

The detective's only clue to the whereabouts of a man on the run is the list of words below. He is hiding in a building in the heart of London. Work out what these words mean and it should guide you to the building where he is concealed. Is it a school, a church, a factory or a theatre?

REIGNS

PERTAIN

STRAIT

CRANED

RESIGNED

ROASTING

CARTHORSE

5

LETSBY AVENUE

In Letsby Avenue there is a large police HQ subdivided into three separate buildings. There is a fourth police building a distance from the others.

Can you divide the map so that each building appears on its own patch and ALL divisions are identical in area and in shape?

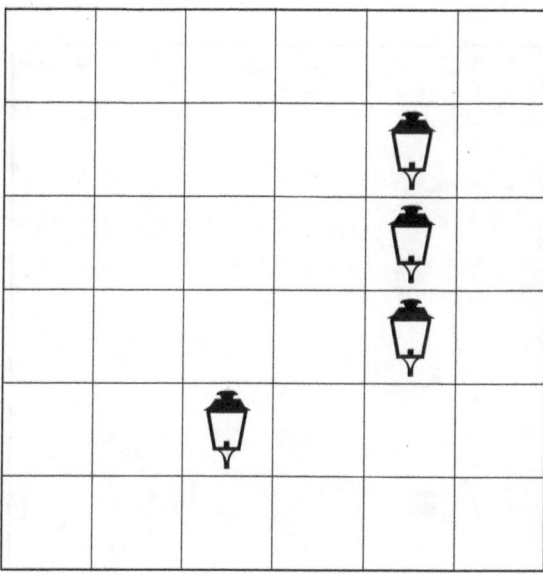

6

ONE WAY SYSTEM

You and your co-driver must make your way through the maze of back streets to reach your destination and catch the thieves red handed. As if the labyrinth of highways and byways wasn't enough, you also have to contend with one way systems. Find the right route and always travel in the direction of the arrows. If the arrow is going towards you as you try and enter a street you must seek an alternative route. You must travel from the top to the bottom of the map. Where will you start, and where will you finish?

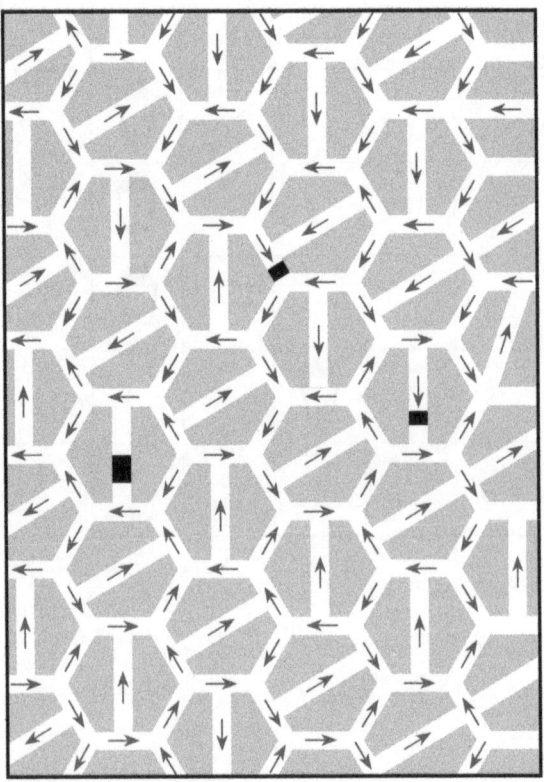

7

PAWNBROKER

Pawnbroking was introduced in England in the thirteenth century. A person could leave a valuable item with the pawnbroker in return for ready cash, with the opportunity to buy the item back at a later date when his or her financial circumstances had improved. Of course, the pawnbroker charged for his services.

Some pawnbrokers were more honest than others. Here are some receipts that the men at the Yard have collected. One of them looks a bit suspicious as it doesn't follow the pattern of the rest. Can you work out which one it is?

| 0 0 |

| 6 9 |

| 8 8 |

| 9 9 |

| 6 0 9 |

| 8 0 8 |

CHAPTER TEN

THE GLOBAL ARM
OF THE LAW

Scotland Yard has always been renowned the world over. Perhaps this is because in the past its take on policing was markedly different from other forces' more oppressive and intrusive approaches. In the late nineteenth century, for example, political radicals from the continent who came to London were astonished to find that the police were not there to follow their every move, beat them up, demand their papers, haul them before magistrates and imprison them. Equally, though, the Yard has always been known for its cutting-edge policing and there were times when authorities in other countries would call upon its expertise to help solve especially baffling riddles connected with ingenious crimes. The Yard's fame and influence has always reached right around the world.

The puzzles in this section involve conundrums set on transcontinental trains and ocean-going ships, as well as whodunnits in capitals across Europe. Indeed, in the days before Interpol (a body that had its origins in the early years of the twentieth century but coalesced into its current form in 1956), Scotland Yard was most assiduous at forging new and productive links with police forces elsewhere. Victorian detectives were faced with a newly interconnected world where villains might sail to distant continents and cross vast land masses by rail. The committed criminal with international ambitions had to be countered by a similarly international network of detectives. This often proved difficult in the early days of Scotland Yard, when long-distance communication was slow and inefficient.

Nonetheless, one of Scotland Yard's most strikingly cosmopolitan figures in the days of gaslights and hansom cabs was Inspector Charles Hagen. He was one of the very first recruits to the newly branded 'CID' in 1878 and his particular speciality was cases involving criminals from abroad. Hagen himself was a man of German heritage and as well as being fluent in German, he was also a superb French speaker. For a time, he had been personal bodyguard to the Prince of Wales, accompanying him as he made visits to continental Europe. In an age of political violence and assassinations, this was not an easy assignment and Hagen was himself once arrested by the Austrian police in Vienna; they had not realised that this man treading so close upon the footsteps of royal dignitaries was there purely for protection.

Back in London, Hagen was a formidable multitasker and a great detective. He once stepped in to aid the Russian ambassador Count Schuvaloff when a young German approached him and offered to sell him secret super-weapons that had the power to stop torpedoes. There were no such weapons and it was clear that the man was a con artist. It was Hagen who traced the man back to his dwellings in a south London suburb, following a trail of German expatriates whom he had swindled.

Then there were the more athletic cases he faced. In one situation he was required to chase a French forger through the tight, winding maze of alleys that lay in the heart of the City of London. The Frenchman thought he had found a hiding place in one of the tucked-away taverns near the Bank of England but the patient Hagen was simply waiting for him to break cover. And once he had brought this variety of continental miscreants to court, Hagen had a further task; very often he would step in to interpret for them. First, he would relay the questions of prosecution and defence and then, for the benefit of the court, he would translate the accused's answers. While no one ever suggested that Hagen was anything other than objective and truthful, the general principle of a detective interpreting the words of the accused was eventually felt to be rather inappropriate.

Another strand of Charles Hagen's working life was the presence in London of a wide variety of hot-headed political revolutionaries.

Exiles from Germany and France would congregate in the smoky taverns of Fitzrovia near Oxford Street, and distribute and sell revolutionary newspapers calling for anarchy and assassination. One such person was Johann Most, who edited a newspaper from an office just behind the Euston Road in the early 1880s. Scotland Yard kept a careful eye on such publications and organisations but did not approach all the eager young anarchists who attended. The police were there to observe fiery speeches in the back rooms of pubs, but it was felt that taking action would be stepping over a boundary into political control, and most of these men weren't a threat. Nonetheless, when Most's newspaper put out a special edition exulting in the violent killing of Tsar Nicholas II, he had taken things too far. Any publications that threatened to bring violence, especially to the streets of London, could not be tolerated. He was arrested, tried, and sentenced to eighteen months in prison; thereafter Most emigrated to America.

In addition, a long time before the official protocols of Interpol, Inspector Charles Hagen was among those who helped set up an intricate network of crime-fighter contacts across Europe. The information stream flowed both ways, with Scotland Yard being alerted to criminals who had escaped custody abroad and were most likely to try and find refuge in London, and foreign forces being informed of offenders who had fled the capital and were known to be making their way to France, Germany, or even America. This cross-border cooperation was also deployed in the solving of some puzzling and ingenious thefts. In 1913, a haul of extremely valuable pearl jewellery was artfully lifted from a sealed box as it was being transported from London to Paris. Here was a crime that exercised the detective minds of both Scotland Yard and its French counterpart, the Sûreté. The ingenuity of the theft was one thing – among the items spirited away were sixty-one pearls that had been replaced with sugar lumps, replicating their weight in the sealed box – but the key mystery was: at what point in the journey had this audacious robbery taken place? On board the first class train compartment to Dover? In the smart suite on the boat that sailed across the Channel? The train set for Paris? The theft was only discovered when the parcel arrived at the Parisian offices of the pearls' owner Max Mayer. The thief or thieves clearly had full knowledge of the itinerary of the sealed box. All items within were safe and accounted for in London, so had the thief been disguised as a train or boat steward? And as the insurance company started clamouring for more information before making a payout, could the police on either side of the Channel agree upon whose territory, and therefore whose responsibility, this was? This rare case seemed insoluble. It seemed unlikely that the haul would be sold at once thus giving the police teams a new lead – as with other successful high-profile robberies, the villains were presumably under no pressure to offload the valuables quickly as the sale of a precious pearl here and there would likely have been enough to keep wolves from the door.

Yet the persistence of Scotland Yard, and detective Alfred Ward, led them to monitor a known and rather suave jewel thief called Joseph Grizzard, and to establish who his contacts and associates were by means of undercover officers. After a long investigation, they sent out trick messages to each gang member telling them to rendezvous at Chancery Lane tube station at a certain time. Grizzard materialised, as did his associates and all were arrested. But there were no pearls to show for the arrest. Astoundingly, they did turn up, though, but as a result of pure chance. In a quiet north London suburb, a piano maker on his way home saw a man stop and very carefully drop an object in the gutter before sprinting off. Intrigued, the piano maker investigated, found a discarded box of matches and opened it: within lay the palely gleaming pearls. The police assumed that another of Grizzard's associates had seen how the Yard was closing in on the gang and, in a panic, tried to get rid of the haul.

But how had Grizzard pulled off the crime in the first place? By targeting one particular link in the journey of the pearls: the Parisian postman who received the package as it arrived at the Gare du Nord station. In return for a large sum of cash, the postman arranged for one of Grizzard's associates to get access alongside him to the package – just for a matter of seconds – and pull off the swap. A clever ruse relying on the fact that no one gave a second glance to men wearing postal uniforms . . .

Away from the glamour of Paris, London was also a deeply attractive destination for a new professional class of criminal. This was partly because the British authorities had never been as zealous as their continental counterparts when it came to all citizens and immigrants carrying documentation and being registered with town halls and police stations. Gangs who had carried out heists on the continent could sail to England and acquire a house, or houses, in which to stash both loot and even gang members. There were lurid reports of houses in London that had hidden staircases and special buttons that rang warning bells in the house next door to alert gang members that they needed to make themselves scarce (though in these newspaper reports, the gang members retained their anonymity).

In the early years of the twentieth century, one enterprising criminal was apprehended by Scotland Yard detectives using a combination of international cooperation and a most amazing new technological innovation: Professor Korn's 'telephotography' apparatus. A young German scientist had formulated a means by which a photograph might be sent by telegraph, arriving hundreds of miles away in just minutes. The technique involved glass cylinders, prisms and a substance called selenium. The idea, a precursor of the principles of television, was considered startlingly brilliant and effective and it worked terrifically well in the case of a chief bank cashier in Stuttgart who had succumbed to temptation and made off with an enormous sum in cash and gold. The German police, with their telephotography apparatus, transmitted the man's photograph to the detectives at Scotland Yard. In a matter of hours, they were able to make multiple copies of the image and then take them to the major railway terminals – Waterloo, Victoria, Charing Cross – that greeted the boat trains from Stuttgart. The thief was horrified when, upon arrival at Charing Cross, he saw officials intently comparing large photographs of him with the faces of disembarking passengers. Escape was futile and all the stolen loot was recovered from his baggage.

The years following First World War saw police cooperation and coordination placed on a new, ambitious, global footing, a web with threads across all continents: the International Criminal Police Congress. Scotland Yard joined in 1928, and after Second World War, the organisation became known as Interpol. From drug smuggling to terrorism, intelligence was beamed instantly across borders. But in individual cases, there was still a certain etiquette to observe within those borders. New York District Attorney Robert Morgenthau recalled a case in the 1980s when US Federal Agents were chasing international arms runners who had pitched up in London; he had to put in calls to ensure that Scotland Yard would allow the US detectives to continue their pursuit in the capital. They were most welcome.

It is pleasing to see that the particular expertise of Scotland Yard is still sought after internationally to this day. Very recently, it was announced that the Yard would be helping out in the matter of treasures robbed from ancient tombs in Egypt and the Sudan. Illicit trade in funerary items from the time of the Pharaohs is still a huge problem and the Yard, with the Egyptian and Sudanese governments and experts from the British Museum, are devising methods by which such trade can be brought to a halt. It is a tribute to Scotland Yard's hard work and ingenuity that the British – who in the early twentieth century had dived into the most sacred sealed tombs and systematically stripped them – are welcome in this trilateral force.

And so the following puzzles reflect that transcontinental feel; reaching out across the world, the long arm of the law is, in the case of Scotland Yard, quite unusually long!

1

CAPITAL OFFENCE

The letters in the names of five capital cities have been replaced by the digits 1-9. The replacement digits are consistent throughout. Can you work out where this international traveller has been.

1 1 2 3 1

2 2 4 1 5 3

3 6 7 5 2 2 4 3 2

4 8 1 3 1 9 6 1

5 7 1 9 4

2

WHERE TO?

The hunt for criminal masterminds had always been a global mission. Look at the message below. How many countries have been investigated in this particular case, and what are they?

A person may linger many a time without arousing suspicion. Carrying out what seems like a normal task may not be normal at all. For example, the church I left yesterday has been a focus of suspicion for a long time. An institution such as a church in a strange way should be above suspicion.

Looking at the trade in guns, a rifle ban on the other hand would be understandable. I can't believe I ran into a rifle dealer purely by accident. One similar gent in another part of the city wouldn't look suspicious. Perhaps it's all in the mind, I anticipate an arrest soon.

3

INTERPOL'S INTERCEPTION

The following message has been intercepted by Interpol. Read it carefully. There are three possible courses of action which you can then take. It is of vital importance you make the right decision. What will it be?

'Jackal is the code name. Feelings must be kept under tight control. Many an operation fails when the heart rules the head. Appear calm at all times. Make your move only when the time is right. Justice must be seen to be carried out. Judge carefully when it is time to act. Augment your back up team if you feel that it is the right time to do so.'

What is your decision?

a) Never return to HQ if you fail!

b) Secret documents are to be destroyed at once!

c) Return to your head office without delay!

4

SAIL AWAY

Your first meeting was on a yacht in Monaco. The second meeting was on a yacht in Nice.

The third meeting was on a yacht in the Bay of Naples. It's hard work, but someone has to do it! The fourth meeting is in Saint-Tropez.

Which of the six yachts is the one you are looking for in Saint-Tropez?

MONACO   NICE

BAY OF NAPLES

SAINT-TROPEZ

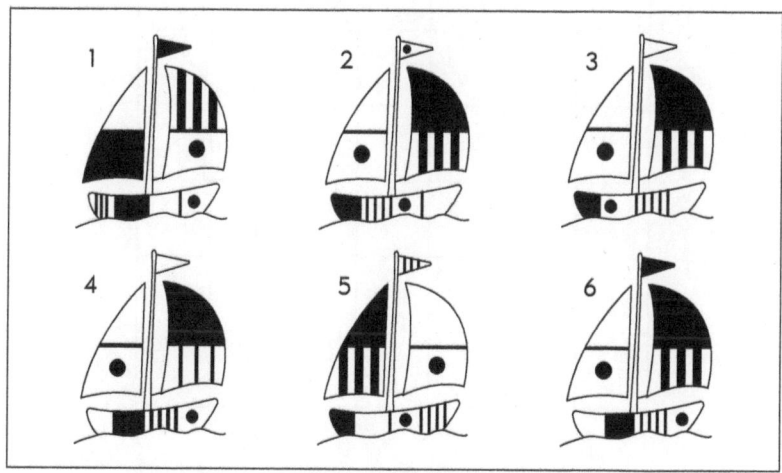

5

MOVING ON

These are the only instructions you receive to help you find your European destination. Look at the seven countries listed below. Write them going across in the grid in such a way that an eighth country is revealed. This is your destination. There is one letter in place to point you in the right direction.

AUSTRIA

BELGIUM

DENMARK

FINLAND

GERMANY

HOLLAND

ICELAND

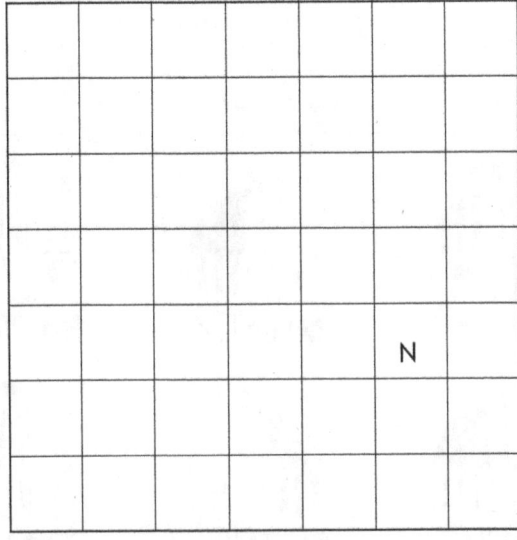

6

INTERLOCKING

There's not much to go on, just a list of three-letter words. They can be fitted together in an intriguing way to make four, six-letter words. The initial letters of those six-letter words spell out your destination. It's a tough one! The only clue we give you is the title of the puzzle. Good luck!

ALE

AND

LID

LUG

ONE

PIE

SET

WAS

CHAPTER ELEVEN

THE YARD
IN THE FUTURE

The police of the future are often painted in quite a sinister light. When science fiction writers and film makers imagine the world to come, the law-enforcers are sometimes robots (*Robocop*); sometimes terrifying and authoritarian magistrates (*Judge Dredd*); or, in the case of one particular alien species featured in *Doctor Who*, space rhinos who act as judge, jury and executioner rolled into one. The real police in Scotland Yard, however, are mindful of concerns that technology is changing the way the law is upheld. There are certainly no plans to introduce space rhinos and, more than that, there is an active belief that no matter how advanced artificial intelligence and robotic innovations become, the principle of the Yard must continue to adhere to Sir Robert Peel's 1829 motto: 'The police are the people'.

Nonetheless, advances in technology have brought the science of detection forward in leaps and bounds. Cold cases of the past have been solved with innovative new technology, and current crimes, performed by the modern-day nifty criminal, are swiftly solved with the forensic analysis available to the force. And so, the puzzles in this section celebrate Scotland Yard in its new age, and task you with all the new challenges facing detectives. We'll see conundrums involving computers and algorithms, and contend with puzzles concerning the power of informed prediction and remote-controlled cityscape surveillance.

Rather like their Victorian counterparts, today's Scotland Yard officers understand that they are standing on the threshold of a completely new landscape – both socially and criminally. The spread of the internet, social media and online transactions are thought by some to constitute a new Industrial Revolution. It is certainly changing the way that criminal gangs operate, and also the scale of their operations, giving them a global access that they never had before. Gangs now have the chance to communicate on wholly encrypted devices, and cheap air travel means fast and easy movement anywhere on the planet. Computer-based frauds make nonsense of national borders. In the old days, crime at least required a physical presence. Now it can be committed remotely from thousands of miles away.

This is why science fiction writers have tended to imagine a police force that responds in kind: a constabulary of super-fast computer operators, able to tap into countless databases, and also able to get ahead by anticipating and parrying further electronic moves. These writers see a day when crimes can be solved before they are even committed. But the reality is much more complex, and more reassuring, than this. A recent conference of senior police personnel, some from Scotland Yard and others from forces around the world, discussed how new policing was to work without being too intrusive into general computer privacy, or too remote from the public on the streets. It was noted, for instance, that the future would see a greater use of drones; small flying devices that can film while nimbly flying through streets. This could pretty much fill the role currently carried out by police helicopters, but more efficiently. How better to track an offender unobtrusively than by sending one of these quiet flying automatons out to hover above with its unblinking eye? Drones have already proved extremely valuable in terms of carrying out searches. People and details that could be missed on foot are captured in high definition by cameras floating just a few feet above the ground.

The increasing use of this technology has raised important questions about what counts as public and private space, because drones see and record everything, not merely a suspect wandering about. They can see into back gardens, and in through doors and windows. Added to this, drones in the future could also be fitted with facial recognition software, which means that the police would have the power to watch and record the movements of everybody, offenders and innocent parties alike, as well as identify them. Because the police, and especially Scotland Yard, have always been sensitive to the idea of muscling in on the private space of the innocent, there is a strong need for the ethics to be debated, and safeguards discussed. In previous decades, the use of phone-tapping, in its day an innovation as useful as drones, caused all sorts of arguments, and Scotland Yard has always been intensely careful about its deployment, and about the rules under which it can be used.

One slightly unexpected development that has come from the computer age is that detectives now arguably have too much evidence. That is, the amount of information that is contained on the phones and computers of suspects is absurdly vast. In some cases, there are just simply not enough officers to be able to digest and analyse all of the data stored. But innovative steps have been taken and experiments carried out; not with humans, but with artificial intelligence, to see if a computer can analyse everything on a device from photos, to documents, to messages, to contacts, at a speed unimaginably faster than any human could manage. Facial recognition software could also alert officers to other gang members who show up in pictures. Again, there are a huge number of legal firepits to fall into here, including how to protect the public against being mistakenly identified by artificial intelligence and also the extent to which messages and closed social media postings can be burrowed into without violating all codes of privacy. But the exciting thing is the principle: for it also cannot be right that gangs get to take full advantage of an electronic world without Scotland Yard having electronic armoury with which to protect the public.

Slightly more troublingly, there are some police forces that are taking tentative steps towards prediction, as depicted in the dystopian science-fiction drama *Minority Report*. In that 2002 film, murders were 'predicted' by figures called 'pre-cogs' (as in pre-cognitive) and those who were envisaged committing the crime in the future were restrained (in the story, the knotty problem of predestination became a paradox: if someone is made aware of the future probability that they will kill, there is the chance they can ensure that they do not carry out the murder, thus eradicating that future and erasing the guilt, so the predicted murderers would be unjustly apprehended). There now exists a form of technology that uses algorithms to predict if an arrested person will offend again. As detectives from any era would recognise, this poses questions not merely about policing but indeed about the foundations of human nature.

If a computer can predict if we are ninety per cent likely to commit a crime, does this mean that there is no such thing as free will? Or worse, does this mean that there is next to no possibility of redemption? It also returns us to the age-old subject of whether a criminal brain is recognisably different from that of a non-offender. Where the Victorians believed in phrenology – the study of cranial bumps and nodules – the modern computer appears to envisage the criminal brain as a series of algorithms, suggesting that a criminal can simply be seen as a pre-programmed machine. Naturally, a great many people have recoiled with some force from this idea. And does it not make the very notion of policing itself redundant? To follow the argument to its natural conclusion: the computer spots and singles out the potential murderer; the potential murderer is arrested and, for his own good, as well as his potential victim, incarcerated. Result: no murders. But how could we ever punish people for crimes they have not actually committed? Ultimately, by allowing computers to decide the probabilities of human behaviour and potential, the most essential freedom is being stripped away from everybody; the chance to change course, the possibility of being a force for good rather than bad. Human brains are not algorithms. For if they were, what exactly would be the point of doing anything at all?

When senior personnel from Scotland Yard and elsewhere had their conference on the future of policing in 2018, there was a strong agreement that the human factor always had to be front and centre. Drones are all very well as all-seeing eyes, but you also need police officers on the streets. And while it is very useful to have a computer that can whizz through millions of texts, you still need human judgement to give all the messages proper context and interpretation.

When it comes to the graver crimes, no amount of computer programming can replicate the work of an experienced detective in interviewing a killer and reassuring the wider community. More than this, no computer can ever unlock the secrets of a criminal's heart. No amount of data analysis can explain the psychological knots that form motive, and there are still crimes behind closed doors – the theft of valuables, or chilling murders – which become complex labyrinths of human compulsion. So, in the immediate future it is highly unlikely that Scotland Yard will be deploying androids in blue uniforms to chase after miscreants at bionic speeds while shooting bright red laser bolts from their eyes.

Indeed, it is more likely that Scotland Yard's future might look and feel a little like the enduring symbol of Britain's greatest contribution to science fiction – the tardis. In *Doctor Who*, the eponymous Time Lord decided to disguise his miraculous space and time machine as a police box. These dark blue structures stood on London's street corners from the late 1940s to the late 1960s. Their function was to act as a handy temporary holding cell for apprehended wrongdoers, as well as providing police with telephones to use in case of emergencies. A few years back, Scotland Yard decided to reintroduce and update the notion of the police box, with a model in Earls Court.

The telephone part of this box has been disused for a little while now, but the structure itself is still a perfect image for the Yard to project into our troubled present: quirky, unexpected, yet also understated and quietly dignified. And as with *Doctor Who*'s craft, it is a structure that conceals a range of potential hidden uses and innovation; until not long ago, it contained disguised CCTV cameras, (funding for the equipment dried up, so currently it is now more of an ornament). On the streets of Glasgow in Scotland, some remaining antique police boxes are treated as public sculptures. Speaking of which, the image of the police box was used a few years ago by the artist Mark Wallinger, who created one composed entirely of mirrored, reflective surfaces, giving a weirdly illusory sense that it was both there and not there at the same time. The point of the police box still remains though: a totem of reassurance that could conceivably contain a live constable having a crafty sit-down with a Thermos flask of tea. Like the revolving sign outside the Scotland Yard headquarters, the Earl's Court police box is a tourist attraction. And it is difficult to imagine the apparatus of police forces in other parts of the world being greeted with such unalloyed affection and delight. One day, such a police box might indeed contain a robot constable. But the aim would always be to make the public feel safe, rather than to intimidate them.

And in this spirit, the puzzles in this section have a flavour of the futuristic: enigmas centred on electronic surveillance and data collection and analysis and lightning fast leaps of logic . . .

1

BLUES IN TWOS

Whatever the future holds for policing there is little doubt that the officers in blue will continue to patrol their beats in pairs. In this puzzle we ask you to look for pairs of a different type.

Complete the words below by adding the first two and the last two letters. In each separate case, the same two letters are needed and they must stay in the same order.

1 _ _ T I Q U A R I _ _

2 _ _ E E P I _ _

3 _ _ R M I N A _ _

4 _ _ E A D F A _ _

5 _ _ L I G H T _ _

6 _ _ P L A N A D _ _

7 _ _ E P S A _ _

8 _ _ I R T I E _ _

9 _ _ I G I N A T _ _

10 _ _ C A P T U _ _

2

FOLLOWING ORDERS

Orders must be followed. But what are the orders? There are instructions in this message that are clear for all who read it. There are also clues in the message to set you on your course to identify the NEXT meeting place. Where is it?

ORIGINAL MESSAGE READS:

Arrive at the station before twelve, noon. Be prepared for it to be busy, as people will be finishing their elevenses. Choose a quiet place to wait, this is often difficult to find. Don't let on that you are a policeman, but of course you are renowned for your canniness. Everyone in the division has been informed and knows about the freight train and its cargo. Forget about all other matters even though it might be tricky. Go to greet the tall man in the green blazer in case he can't identify you via some sixth sense. He will be wearing dark glasses, if I've had my orders followed to the letter. I advise remaining on the main platforms and one of our men will be waiting. Just be careful and take the right path, re-entering the station if needs be.

Where is your meeting place?

a) Marble Arch at 4 p.m.

b) Knightsbridge Underground at 5 p.m.

c) King's Cross station at 2 p.m.

d) London Bridge at 3 p.m.

3

SWIPE CARD

Look at the symbols on the swipe cards below, these indicate which hotel room number the key will open. There are SEVEN symbols in all, each represents a number between 1 and 7.

←···	···→	↑	←···	←···	=	9
↔	↔	↕	←···	···→	=	14
···→	←···	↓	···→	↔	=	15
ϟ	←···	···→	↓	···→	=	18
↓	←···	↓	↑	←···	=	20
···→	↓	←···	↓	ϟ	=	23

Which room number will swipe card ϟ ϟ ↔ ···→ ↕ open?

193

4

THE POWER OF OBSERVATION

Technology has evolved beyond many people's wildest dreams. Yet when you are dealing with people, observation is still key, making links is vital and remembering what you have seen is a powerful skill.

Look at the shapes below. You will see that they all look very different. However there are two shapes that are the same. Having seen one can you remember it and match it with the other?

5

DOWNLOAD THE APP

Look at the fragments of messages below. Clearly there are some words missing and the number of dashes in these words indicates the number of missing letters. If you need further assistance, all we can say is 'download the app!'

1 In the theatre, the _ _ _ _ _ _ _ _ was deafening as people
   _ _ _ _ _ _ _ their hands and stamped their feet. There was
   a wonderful _ _ _ _ _ _ _ between the performer and the
   audience. As the mystery figure _ _ _ _ _ _ _ _ _ _ _ the
   stage, the lights dimmed, and a _ _ _ _ _ _ _ sound was
   heard. No one would have willingly _ _ _ _ _ _ _ seats at
   that chilling moment.

2 The jewel raid _ _ _ _ _ _ _ _ to be an open and
   shut case. The precious _ _ _ _ _ _ _ _ _ _, carefully
   _ _ _ _ _ _ _ in a velvet bag, _ _ _ _ _ _ _ _ _ _ _ _ as
   if into thin air. Their owner had made an emotional
   _ _ _ _ _ _ for their safe return. Maybe the robbery had
   left him _ _ _ _ _ _ _ _ for cash. No one has as yet
   been _ _ _ _ _ _ _ _ _ _ _, and no one knows what will
   _ _ _ _ _ _ next.

3 The young _ _ _ _ _ _ _ was not at all _ _ _ _ _ _ (that
   rhymes!). He had completely lost his _ _ _ _ _ _ _ _ _,
   and was refusing food. Fruit, his usual favourite,
   whether it be traditional English _ _ _ _ _ _, or
   tropical _ _ _ _ _ _ _ _ _ _, did not meet with his
   _ _ _ _ _ _ _ _ _, and he _ _ _ _ _ _ _ at those who
   tried to tempt him. Perhaps a different _ _ _ _ _ _ _ _ was
   needed.

6

KEYPAD

The cyber criminal has tapped out a message regarding an important rendezvous. As you can see from the phone keypad each number can be any one of three or four letters. Using your powers of deduction and ingenuity can you work out which letter is represented by each number, and therefore decode the message.

4   226   733   968   66   843   53889 · 43
968   9268.   47   6666   86667769   65?   4
4673   76.

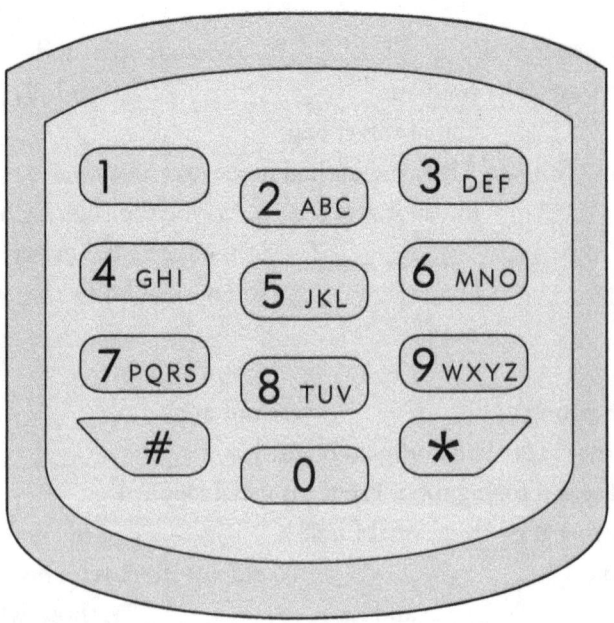

7

THE PERFECT PASSCODE

There are many ways of remembering passcodes, some more ingenious than others. Ruby Diamond had a fabulous jewellery collection. Most of it was kept in a safe with a nine digit passcode, ending in a nine, which was quite difficult to remember. One day Ruby arrived at her favourite restaurant wearing a beautiful triangular shaped necklace, which was admired by one and all. What those admirers didn't know was that on the back of the necklace there were lots of numbers, which seemed to be written at random. But Ruby was no fool. She had created a unique way of remembering the passcode to her safe. It could be found by going from the wide end of the necklace to the narrow end, picking up a different number each time, on one level at a time, until the nine at the bottom was reached. All the numbers 1 to 9 were used.

What was Ruby's perfect passcode?

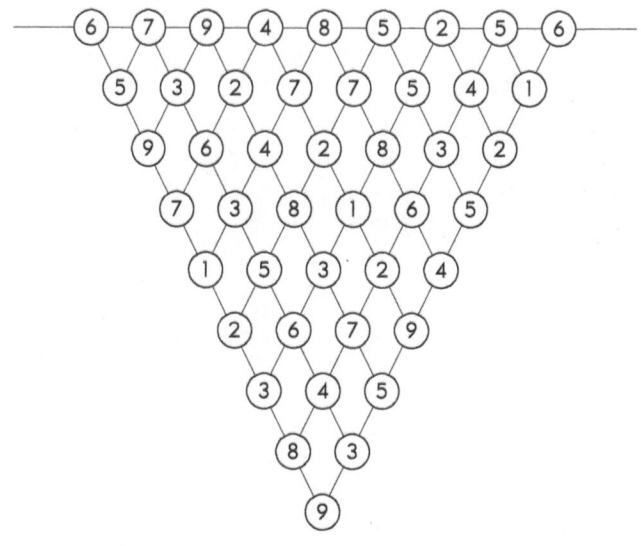

CHAPTER TWELVE

THE FINAL CHALLENGE

The process of becoming a detective takes much more than picking up a magnifying glass and applying a shrewd eye, it involves a huge amount of focus and application. You might be preternaturally talented when it comes to reading a room for significant details, or untangling knots of contradictions between different testimonies, but you still need to understand the law to ensure that it is upheld. Instinct must be supported by knowledge, and action supported by planning.

So among the puzzles in this section are vintage questions from real Metropolitan Police examinations back in the 1930s, a taste of the sort of vigorous selection procedures that were carried out then, and indeed now.

Though, funnily enough, Scotland Yard has very recently mooted a new approach to recruiting and training detectives: a twelve-week fast-track course aimed at graduates. Most potential detectives have to serve many years in uniform before promotion, in line with tradition stretching back to the nineteenth century. This is because police officers who work a long time on the force form an intimate understanding not only of certain locales, but also of how to deal with people who are under intense stress; victims of crime and offenders too. These constables on the beat acquire an essential judgement despite not having the powers to investigate crimes beyond the initial stages. They learn how to read the non-verbal signals of potentially violent people and they develop a sharp nose for deceit in all of its forms.

To reach the position of Detective Constable, on the traditional route through the ranks, one must complete a series of hard exams.

The candidate is given three months to revise from set law texts and then must sit papers which feature a number of complex hypothetical criminal scenarios, all while continuing normal shifts out on the streets. Here is a simplified example:

Two muggers tell their female target to hand over her bag; she refuses and a struggle breaks out. The woman fights one of the muggers furiously, but in doing so, she slips and falls and hits her head on a paving stone. She is taken to hospital. A few days later the injury proves fatal. You must choose from four or five options to determine the precise legal extent the muggers are responsible for their victim's death. Is one more responsible than the other? Should one or both be charged?

The answer, incidentally, is that as the law currently stands both the muggers hold responsibility and both should face charges accordingly.

Things get trickier and even more intensely detailed when aiming for the positions of Detective Sergeant and Detective Inspector. There are manuals to digest, and they are not light reading. So what keeps candidates pushing for these positions? Well, all this hard work is balanced against the promise of a career that not only helps countless people, but also gives an extraordinary insight into worlds most of us will never see.

Just as the Scotland Yard detectives of yesteryear frequently plunged into rookeries and labyrinthine slums in pursuit of offenders from gang leaders to murderers, so today's officers must weave their way through elaborate networks of crime. They must navigate large estates with highly organised drug-selling rings and wealthy suburbs with crime-lord residents who are covertly directing operations carried out by those further down the chain.

And curiously, despite the digital age ensuring that every single microscopic detail is instantly preserved and can be flashed up on screens almost in an instant – a single fingerprint eliciting a thousand file photographs, whittled down in a flash to the corresponding mug shot – the role of the detective is much as it has been since Inspector Jack Whicher inspected those Road House linen cupboards in 1860.

The heavy police manuals on training and points of law teach the vital framework upon which justice rests. But no manual nor digital camera nor artificial intelligence programme can yet talk to a suspect and instantly register the subtleties of their non-verbal responses. No computer can look at a warren of passageways leading through a 1970s housing estate and instantly size up the potential hiding places, and the possible danger spots. And, especially when dealing with tragedies, there is nothing that can bring the comfort that police officers provide to people who are suffering previously unimaginable traumas. This might be an age of instant gratification, but for the detective, results are not instant. There are investigative strands to follow, suspects to chase down and unexpected avenues of questioning opened up by curious witness statements.

All that said, the manuals and the exams and the computers are invaluable. For the other philosophical strand that runs all the way through the history of Scotland Yard is that its detectives are not individualistic mavericks or loners seeking to take justice into their own hands. We must put aside the popular fictional image of the investigator who prefers operas and crosswords to human company, or who has too sharp a taste for drink. The true ethos of Scotland Yard has always been that it is collaborative.

The care that was once taken with cross-referenced little cards in wooden filing drawers has (thankfully) given way to incredibly sophisticated computer databases. The presence of police constables walking the streets and having sneaky cups of tea inside their snug police boxes has morphed into countless CCTV cameras on every street and alley that are monitored by careful eyes in a central control room. The ingenuity of Sir Bernard Spilsbury's 'murder kit', devised so that detectives might not taint evidence, has evolved into technology that has astounding sensitivity to every single strand of DNA. Throughout the years, though, there has always been that sense of a team. The detectives of the Yard were never heading out into the streets to face criminals alone; they were always supported by their colleagues.

It remains the case today that in many parts of the world Scotland Yard is revered and applauded. Many people cannot imagine living in a country where the police are there purely and simply to protect you rather than to monitor your political beliefs, or to oppress you in other ways. From this point of view, the Scotland Yard bobby and detective both stand as emblems of the most extraordinary ideal: a society living under a rule of law that is upheld with care and dignity.

The fogs of popular imagination never quite seem to disperse either. Scotland Yard will always carry associations with stout constables, moustaches twitching, and lean detectives, adjusting their trilby hats in the darkness. And happily, what these figures will always project is that most vital part of all detective work: fair play. Holmes and all the other fictional detectives may be heroes on paper – but the women and men of the real-life Scotland Yard deserve our deepest admiration too.

THE FINAL CHALLENGE PUZZLES

There might be some who argue that when it comes to detecting skills, there is no substitute for hard-earned experience. But even the wisest men and women in uniform have to be tested somehow, to demonstrate that they are ready to enter the labyrinths of the criminal mind. An episode of the popular television drama *Endeavour* that features the exploits of a young Inspector Morse depicts the Detective Sergeant in the 1960s sitting an examination in a hall. He finishes the paper with extraordinary speed, turning thereafter to his crossword. But what sort of exam questions did aspiring detectives actually face?

In this section, we present an array of questions, drawn from real Scotland Yard exam papers. These questions hail from the 1930s, so as well as showing what would-be detectives had to think about when solving crimes, they provide an intense flavour of the pre-war period (Indeed, one or two questions in those exam booklets could not be reproduced now as they contained wildly outdated terms). Of course, these exam problems were not intended as escapist puzzles, but now they can definitely be approached in that way. Think of them more as a sort of common sense challenge. Indeed, the senior detectives who were marking the candidates' answers back in the 1930s were looking not merely for precise legal knowledge, but also for flashes of lateral thinking and initiative.

Delightfully, deep in the archives we also uncovered a snappy visual test along with the questions. This is a 1930s challenge for the would-be detective, who is given a few seconds to look at a drawing of a street and remember as many of its details as possible, before answering questions about that scene purely from memory in a few minutes.

This is very much a pencil-and-paper section and you definitely don't need legal training to work out these problems! Guesses are permissible, and answers that are approximate and common-sensical can still count. It might also be fun to answer the questions – exam conditions! – alongside friends and family.

QUESTION 1: (FROM 1938)

You are on Oxford Street at 8.30 p.m. when two obviously respectable but excited ladies approach you. The information you receive from them is to the following effect:

They were looking into the windows of Selfridges when a man – now walking hurriedly away from you – came up to the ladies and seizing one by the arm said: 'I am a Detective Sergeant. I have been watching you for a long time and I am arresting you.' He then led her along the street. She protested and asked what offence she had committed as did also her companion. When they had gone some distance the man said: 'You seem to be a decent woman – what is it worth if I let you go? I am sure you do not want to spend the night in a cell.'

On your approach, the man released the woman and hurried away.

State in detail what you would do; what advice you would give; and what offence, if any, has been committed.

QUESTION 2: (FROM 1938)

You are in Belgrave Square at midnight. An acting sergeant and a police constable cyclist are about 30 yards away. You hear screams and cries for help. A lady rushes out of a house and informs you that her husband is behaving like a madman. He is in a room on the first floor. On entering the room, you see the husband. He is smashing china, furniture, etc. with a poker. There is an empty whisky bottle and a broken tumbler on the floor. It is obvious that the man is not sane, and you suspect delirium tremens. The man's wife says to you: 'My husband has been worried about business and recently he has been drinking heavily. I cannot go on like this. I can do nothing with him, and there are no male servants in the house. Our doctor has suggested male nurses but I cannot agree to that; will you do what is necessary?'

What action would you take?

QUESTION 3: (FROM 1938)

A) A woman is dying in hospital and desires to give information respecting a case of robbery with which two prisoners are charged.

B) A doctor telephones to the police station and says he is at the house of a woman who is suffering from poisoning and not likely to recover. She desires to give information about the person who administered the poison to her.

What action would you take in each case?

QUESTION 4: (FROM 1938)

While on patrol at 10.45 p.m. on a Friday night, you receive information that drinking is going on in a public house, permitted hours being up until 10.30 p.m.. With a PC, you enter the saloon bar and find four men seated at a table on which is bread and cheese for each of them. In front of two of the men are glasses approximately half filled with beer and you see the licensee handing a full glass of beer to each of the other two men.

Who, out of the five persons mentioned, is committing offences? State what these offences are, and the procedure to deal with them.

QUESTION 5: (FROM 1938)

You notice two youths, about 16 years of age, examining a motor car which is standing with the engine running outside a grocer's shop. One of the youths tries the door to ascertain if it is unlocked. The door opens and they both get into the vehicle which is set in motion. You immediately call on the youths to stop and then they admit that they do not know to whom the car belongs and in explanation of their action, say that they were only going for a short ride and had no intention of stealing the car. At that moment a lady leaves the grocer's shop and on seeing you states that she is the owner of the car.

State what action you would take.

QUESTION 6: (FROM 1938)

During a late turn on a summer evening a man is knocked down in a quiet lane by a two-seater motor car which does not stop. Two women walking along the lane at the time witness the incident, note the index number (nb the licence plate) of the car and call a local doctor who, on arrival, pronounces life to be extinct and then telephones the police.

You attend the scene of the accident and ascertain from the two women that the car was being driven by a man accompanied by a young woman passenger. The only description they can give you of the occupants is that the driver was about 40 years of age and was wearing a brown boiler suit and that the woman passenger had red hair.

Having traced the registered owner of the car, you find he has no knowledge of his car having been out since lunchtime. On going with him to his private garage, you find that the car is missing.

The deceased is unknown in the locality and nothing is found on his clothing to give any clue as to his identity.

What steps would you take to trace the driver of the car and to establish the identity of the deceased?

QUESTION 7: (FROM 1938)

A man calls at a shop and obtains goods by representing (that is, pretending) that he has been sent by a customer. He gives the tradesman a cheque purporting to be signed by that customer in payment of the goods and receives a balance in cash. The cheque is returned to the tradesman, who is told that it is a forgery and that the form was obtained from a stolen cheque book. The man is described as: short, fair, well-dressed, middle finger missing from right hand.

What offences have been committed and what action would you take?

QUESTION 8: (FROM 1935)

During the evening of August bank holiday Monday, a respectable middle-aged widow, residing alone in a semi-detached suburban villa is discovered lying dead on the carpeted floor of her dining room. It was murder without a doubt, and death was due to hammer blows to her head, one blow penetrating to the brain. There were no signs of a struggle. No weapons or obvious clue could be found in an ordinary search. The hole in the skull was undoubtedly caused by a hammer, but such a weapon was not in the house. The various rooms had been ransacked in such a manner as to indicate that the murderer only looked for money, but it was known that he only found about £2 10 shillings in notes and silver. There were no finger prints and no marks of forcible entry. No one was seen to enter or leave the house. No screams or noise of a quarrel or struggle were heard by the neighbours. There was little if any splashing of blood.

You are in charge of the investigation. Report what you would do, and why.

QUESTION 9: (FROM 1937)

You are in the street when a man, 'Mr C', a stranger, complains to you that a few minutes earlier in a nearby street a young man who he describes, tried to sell him obscene picture postcards at a shilling each. Assuming that 'Mr C' is able to point out the young man to you, state shortly what action you would take.

QUESTION 10: (FROM 1935)

You are in the street when you are requested to arrest a man for assault. The circumstances are as follows:

'Mr A' alleges that 'Mr B' knocked at his door, and forced his way into his house, and that during the course of the struggle, 'Mr B' struck 'Mr A' on the eye, cutting his eyebrow. 'Mr A''s eyebrow is bleeding freely.

'Mr B', who is quite quiet, denies the assault, and states that his wife had left him two days before, of her own accord. There is no separation order. He saw her enter 'Mr A's house and he has reason to believe 'Mr A' enticed her away. He knocked at the door, which was opened by 'Mr A' and, although the passage was dark, he saw his wife enter a room where there was a light. On entering his house with the intention of speaking to his wife, 'Mr A' tried to prevent him and struggled with him. He did not strike 'Mr A' or attempt to do so, but when they got into the room where his wife was, he saw that 'Mr A''s eyebrow was bleeding badly. He says the injury must have been caused by collision with the door or elsewhere during the struggle in the passage.

'Mrs B' alleges she witnessed the assault. The passage is unlighted. All parties are known to each other. You are not a witness. 'Mr A' insists on charging.

What action would you take, in view of the injury and the whole of the circumstances? Give your view of the circumstances, and your considered reasons for your action.

QUESTION 11: (FROM 1935)

'M' calls at a house to sell stationery. 'Mrs P', an aged woman, answers the door. She refuses to purchase anything. 'M' gets his foot in the doorway and threatens to give 'Mrs P' 'something to remember' with a heavy stick that he is carrying. 'Mrs P' has a weak heart and dies apparently of fright.

What offences have been committed here and what charges should be brought?

QUESTION 12: (FROM 1937)

'Mr X' is employed at a secret government establishment and is found to have taken to his home certain important top secret documents to which he did not legally have access in the course of his work and which would be useful to an enemy. He refuses to make any statement and you are not able to find any proof that he has passed or intended to pass the information to an unauthorised person.

Upon searching his person and house, the only item of interest found is a diary which, among other things, contains a name and address which Military Intelligence say are those of a foreign agent.

Does this in any way alter the complexion of the case? Explain how.

State the offence and outline your action from the time the documents are found by you in 'Mr X''s possession.

QUESTION 13: (FROM 1937)

A young lady, aged 22, of good character, attended a public dance. She consented to dance with a man about her own age who was a complete stranger. Shortly after midnight the young lady accepted the invitation of the young man to drive her home in a motor. When the car reached a spot near her home, she acquainted the young man of this fact; he stopped the car and commenced to pay advances to her in which he attempted to kiss her and placed his hand on her legs.

She repulsed him and attempted to alight but found that she could not open the car door. While she was struggling with the handle of the door the young man drove on at a fast pace. The young lady became more alarmed and, at a spot two or three miles further on, the car slowed down to about 25 miles per hour. The young lady again attempted to open the door and this time succeeded. Being still alarmed and notwithstanding the fact that the young man had made no further attempt to interfere with her, she threw herself out and fell on the roadway. The young man drove on.

A bus conductor took the index number (licence plate) of the car and a pedestrian saw her fall out of the car.

As a result of her fall, the young lady received injuries which although necessitating hospital treatment were not serious enough for her to be detained, but at the same time she was ill for a week.

The case is not reported to Police until a fortnight after the event. Assume you are a Detective Sergeant and are directed to deal with the case: report everything that you would do.

QUESTION 14:
THE VISUAL TEST (FROM 1938)

The drawing which you have just seen illustrates the scene of a smash and grab raid on a shop named Selfridge. Study this scene for one and a half minutes, taking in as much detail as you can. No notes! Then cover the image and address the questions. For these, you have five minutes.

i) The locality, date and time the raid occurred.

ii) By whom were the ground floor premises adjoining Selfridge occupied?

iii) Was there a business motor van in the vicinity at the time of the raid? If so, in what road was it standing and to what firm did it belong?

iv) Was there a dance taking place on the evening on which the raid took place? If so, where was it being held?

v) A car was being driven up Elm Road at the time of the raid. What was the registration number of the car, and how many people were in it?

CONCLUSION

On a foggy night down near the old Jewellery Quarter, cobbles glisten under gaslight. There's a chill in the air, and footsteps echo through the streets. Amid the dark warehouses stands a cheerful corner pub, from which piano music can be heard every time the door opens.

Then: the shrill note of a whistle, piercing through the night.

The whistle is unmistakeable, but the mind wanders to its reasoning . . . Robbery? Murder?

Anything feels possible on such a misty, chilly night.

The truth is that no evocation of London is ever quite complete without the materialisation of a traditional policeman. And more, that policeman should be wearing the most traditional of garb: highly polished, thick-soled shoes; perfectly pressed dark-blue uniform; and that particularly distinctive helmet, which is properly known as a custodian helmet, first introduced in 1863.

The custodian helmet was never that useful as a protective garment, any determined wrongdoer could dent it with enough force, but it has a distinctly recognisable appearance. The tall hat, with the silver badge of the Metropolitan Police proudly affixed to the front, is easy to recognise from wherever you are, in whatever country you might reside. The image of the British bobby is fixed as part of a national character: incorruptible, implacable in pursuit and fundamentally wise in judgement. As puzzle addicts bring order and meaning to scattered clues, so the men and women of the Metropolitan Police piece back normality after the chaos and anarchy of crime.

From constables to detectives, there is an unfazed approach to the enigmas of human nature and an unrelenting determination to map out the maze of motivation that leads to the true perpetrators.

The officers and detectives at Scotland Yard bring together that incredible combination of logic and experience that allows them to get work done. In this ever-changing technological world, science has advanced the means of detection beyond all expectation. Yet, the work of the Scotland Yard in principle remains the same. Whether it be a macabre murder, an audacious theft or a wily heist, detectives must find the clues, collect the evidence and piece together the puzzle.

Detectives know that there is no puzzle so diabolical that it cannot be solved as long as you are committed to see it through to its end. The skills required: relentless energy, a sharp eye, and the ability to look at the world from a lateral tilt. Sometimes, at first glance, puzzles might look incredibly simple, but then reveal themselves to have the greatest depth of complexity. Other conundrums require great leaps and jumps in cognitive thought in order to decrypt and find the answer. Either way, there is always a solution, and once you get to it, you have the same satisfying feeling as when a detective solves a case.

In any given generation – now just as much as when Scotland Yard opened in 1829 – there have been men and women determined to solve the apparently insoluble. Whether using DNA or magnifying glasses or very simply a shrewd eye for the quirks of human nature, recruits to Scotland Yard have always had, and will always have, that insatiable appetite for answers.

FURTHER READING

Ascoli, David, *The Queen's Peace: The Origins and Development of the Metropolitan Police 1829-1979* (Hamish Hamilton, 1979)

Cherrill, Frederick R., *Triumphs of Scotland Yard: A Century of Detection* (J Long, 1955)

Fabian, Robert, *Fabian of the Yard: An Intimate Record* (British Book Centre, 1953)

Mason, Gary, *The Official History of the Metropolitan Police* (Carlton, 2004)

Thomason, Sir Basil, *The Story of Scotland Yard* (Grayson and Grayson, 1935)

ANSWERS

CHAPTER ONE

WHAT HAVE WE HERE?

1

ON THE FRONT LINE

1 BATTLE, **2** HALF, **3** LIFE, **4** POST, **5** SEA, **6** TEST, **7** BACK, **8** DOWN, **9** GREEN, **10** MOUTH.

2

SAFE NUMBER

5 2 7 4 1 6 3.

For the penultimate number to be twice the value of the final number the options are: 2 and 1, 4 and 2, 6 and 3. In the first option the difference between numbers is not greater than one. In option two, it is no longer possible to create the code sequence without odd digits being next to each other. 6 and 3 must be the two final digits. The fifth digit has to be an odd one. 5 and 7 do not give a difference greater than one. Therefore the fifth digit has to be a 1. The fourth digit must be even, and as the difference between adjacent digits is always greater than one, it cannot be a 2. It has to be 4. The number in front of it must be odd and greater than one. Therefore it has to be 7. And so, 2 goes before 7, and 5 must be the first digit.

3

ON YOUR BIKE

Bike 1 appears in 13 rectangles.
Bike 2 appears in 10 rectangles.

Bike 1: ABCDEF, ABCDEFGHI, ACD, ACDG, CD, CDE, CDEF, CDEGH, CDEFGHI, CDG, D, DE, DEF.

Bike 2: ABCDEFGHI, BEFHI, CDEFGHI, CDEGH, EFHI, EH, GH, GHI, H, HI.

4

HIDDEN GEMS

1 Opal, **2** Pearl, **3** Garnet, **4** Diamond, **5** Ruby, **6** Peridot.

5

POST HASTE

18.
That's two more than
the present arrangement.

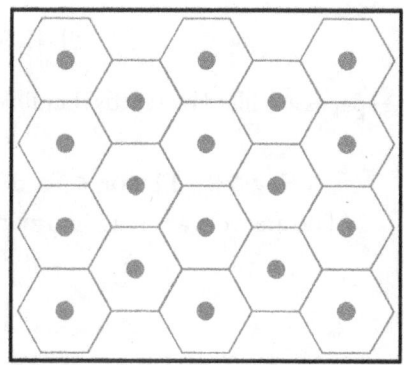

6

WEB OF INTRIGUE

1 Cage, 2 Oval, 3 Verb, 4 Ends, 5 Need, 6 Tune.
The location is Covent Garden.

7

KEY QUESTION

Keys 3 and 7 are identical.

8

CHEERS!

Take the glass fourth from the left. Pour the contents into the empty glass on the far left, making sure not to touch the glass that is being filled. Replace your glass to the position fourth from the left. That's it. Job done!

9

LINKS

The spaces are filled by words that link the given two words together.

1 Key, 2 By, 3 Door, 4 To, 5 Bed, 6 Room, 7 One.
The answers are read in order to reveal the message.

10

SHEER SKULDUGGERY

1 Incorrectly. **2** A postage stamp. **3** Zero. If nine had their own helmets then the tenth must have had theirs as well. **4** The man is given a glass of water. H_2O is the chemical formula for water, and he asked for H to O! **5** Book numbering has the odd numbers on the right hand page and the even numbers on a left hand page. Therefore you could not fit a banknote between pages 5 and 6.

CHAPTER TWO

HUE AND CRY

1

THE BODY SNATCHERS

1 Hip, **2** Chin, **3** Rib, **4** Lip, **5** Heel, **6** Gland, **7** Toe, **8** Leg.

2

A BONE TO PICK

D, K, F, G, B, I, E, A, J, C, H.

3

HUE AND CRY

Adam and Eve, Antony and Cleopatra, Burke and Hare, Crime and Punishment, David and Goliath, Dombey and Son, Gilbert and Sullivan, Holmes and Watson, Jack and Jill, Jekyll and Hyde, Law and Order, Live and Learn, Nuts and Bolts, Oxford and Cambridge, Pen and Ink, Pony and Trap, Romeo and Juliet, Romulus and Remus, Victoria and Albert, Warts and All.

The word left over is TIME.

4

ALL CLUED UP

Across: 1 Tactics, 5 Maths, 8 Alias, 9 Formula, 10 Nobody, 12 Jotted, 13 Eager, 14 Dark, 15 Opal, 17 Thief, 19 Sought, 21 Liners, 24 Suspect, 25 Drama, 26 Dated, 27 Present.

Down: 1 Train, 2 Climber, 3 Inside, 4 Safe, 5 Mirror, 6 Trust, 7 Scandal, 11 Yacht, 12 Jewel, 14 Disused, 16 Prepare, 17 Thread, 18 Fiddle, 20 Upset, 22 Smart, 23 Stop.

5

VOWEL PLAY

1 Whitechapel, 2 Mile End, 3 Notting Hill, 4 Hackney, 5 Bethnal Green, 6 Bow.

6

SHADY CHARACTER

1 Rescues, 2 Fighter, 3 Obtains, 4 Avarice, 5 Dialect, 6 General, 7 Missile, 8 Gladden, 9 Abridge, 10 Process, 11 Smokier, 12 Receded, 13 Toenail, 14 Himself.

The eminent Victorian is Charles Dickens. The shady character is Bill Sikes, gang member and murderer in Charles Dickens's *Oliver Twist*.

7

IN-FILL-TRATE

1 All, **2** For, **3**, One, **4** And, **5** One, **6** For, **7** All.

8

THE MURDER MUSEUM

The murderer is in charge of Room 305.

The shapes are in fact the numbers 3, 7, 0, 9, 5, 8, 1, 4, 2, 6 presented in mirror image form. The splayed hand has deliberately indicated the 3, the 0 and the 5. The fourth finger did not touch the wall as that would have left marks above the 7.

CHAPTER THREE

THE TEST TUBE TRIUMPHS

1

A TO Z OF CRIME

	D		U		Y				J		W		G	
N	U	A	N	C	E		K		E	V	A	D	E	D
	B		I		A		N		W		L		T	
M	I	S	F	O	R	T	U	N	E		L	E	T	S
	O		O		S		C		L		E		I	
Q	U	E	R	Y		S	K	E	L	E	T	O	N	S
	S		M		H		L		E		S		G	
			V	O	Y	E	U	R	S					
	R		C		M		D		Y		F		A	
T	E	N	A	C	I	O	U	S		B	O	B	B	Y
	C		L		C		S		P		R		E	
Z	E	A	L		I	N	T	E	R	C	E	P	T	S
	I		B		D		E		O		M		T	
O	P	P	O	S	E	R		X	R	A	Y	E	D	
	T		X		S				Y		N		D	

225

2

ON THE LEVEL

The levels in 6 and 8 are incorrect. The level in each tube must be at the level of the linked feeder tubes. Tube 6 should be at the same level as the container on the far right. Tube 8 should be the same level as the container on the far left.

3

MEMORABLE MESSAGE

1 Station, **2** Rescued, **3** America, **4** Overrun, **5** Hexagon, **6** Longbow, **7** Gliding, **8** Pimento, **9** Canvass, **10** Glasgow.

The message in the lower grid reads: Travelling as Mr and Master Robinson.

The words are the final part of a message sent by Captain Kendall of the SS Montrose to Scotland Yard in July 1910. It was the first time wireless telegraphy had been used from a ship at sea to apprehend a criminal. The criminal in question was Dr Hawley Crippen, suspected of his wife's murder, who was travelling to Canada with his mistress Ethel Le Neve, disguised as Dr Crippen's son.

4

HOURGLASS

Start both timers. When the smaller of the timers runs out after five minutes, turn it over and let it start again. The larger timer still has four minutes before it runs out. Turn the smaller hourglass over again. Four minutes of sand will have run into the lower area when the larger timer has run out at nine minutes. Turn the smaller hourglass once more. When it is finished the target of thirteen minutes will have been reached.

5

ELEMENTARY

1 Fe: Iron, **2** Al: Aluminium, **3** Na: Sodium,
4 Ag: Silver, **5** He: Helium.

6

CROSS EXAMINE

Across: 8 Almanac, 9 Taper, 10 Solve, 11 Diagram, 12 Ways, 13 Tungsten, 16 Recorded, 18 Jail, 21 Learned, 23 Asked, 25 Steal, 26 Gambler.

Down: 1 Laws, 2 Employ, 3 Index, 4 Acid, 5 Strange, 6 Spirit, 7 Criminal, 12 Wireless, 14 Use, 15 Wrongly, 17 Chased, 19 Alkali, 20 Harms, 22 Digs, 24 Dark.

7

WHAT'S YOUR POISON?

1 Arsenic, **2** Cyanide, **3** Deadly Nightshade,
4 Monkshood, **5** Hemlock.

8

FOOTPRINTS

A is from pair 6.
B from pair 4.
C from pair 2.
D from pair 5.

There are no prints for pair 1 or pair 3.

CHAPTER FOUR

STORMING THE CITADEL

1

FIND THE LADY

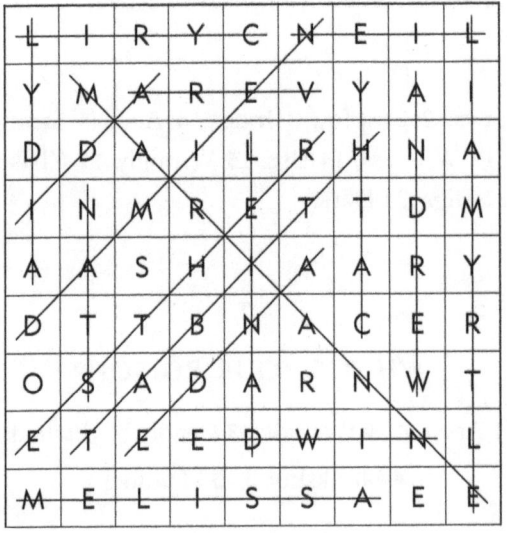

Unused letters are S, O, R, E. The name of the lady is ROSE.

2

OFF THE RECORD

Across: 7 Retail, 8 Feller, 10 Mobster, 11 Toast, 12 Then, 13 Store, 17 Porch, 18 Solo, 22 Crowd, 23 Elastic, 24 Praise, 25 Bearer.

Down: 1 Primate, 2 Stables, 3 Birth, 4 Leotard, 5 Cloak, 6 Grate, 9 Protected, 14 Boldest, 15 Hooters, 16 Concert, 19 Scope, 20 Moral, 21 Laser.

3

DIARY DATES

Each sentence is an anagram. The numbers specifiy the number of letters in the newly formed words. On Monday Pearl's message was: Touring Rome. Hotel suite seven. Grand Hotel.

On Thursday it was: Destination at three. Leaning Tower of Pisa.

4

MULTI TASKING

A: 1 Solve, 2 Haste, 3 Agile, 4 Rogue, 5 Olive, 6 Nerve, 7 Knife, 8 Elope, 9 Route, 10 Range.

B: 1 Joint, 2 Agent, 3 Night, 4 Exact, 5 Might, 6 Alert, 7 Right, 8 Plant, 9 Leapt, 10 Event.

Grid A spells out Sharon Kerr, the first female head of the Flying Squad.

Grid B spells out Jane Marple, Agatha Christie's sleuth from St Mary Mead.

5

NEEDLEPOINT

The rose motif suggests the rose garden. Lady Rosa has embroidered her message with Roman numerals substituted for the letters of the alphabet. It reads: Look inside the sundial.

Full substitution alphabet would read:

A	B	C	D	E	F	G	H	I	J	K
I	II	III	IV	V	VI	VII	VIII	IX	X	XI

L	M	N	O	P	Q	R	S	T	U	V
XII	XIII	XIV	XV	XVI	XVII	XVIII	XIX	XX	XXI	XXII

W	X	Y	Z
XXIII	XIV	XXV	XXVI

6

LADIES DAY

Barbara Black was the lady in the green dress. Barbara Black wore a white hat, green dress and brown shoes. Betty Brown wore a black hat, white dress and green shoes. Gill Green wore a brown hat, black dress and white shoes. Wendy White wore a green hat, brown dress and black shoes.

7

PHONE LINES

1 Jenny D Ext 594. **2** Denise A Ext 548.
3 Lynda C Ext 256. **4** Shirley B Ext 438.

CHAPTER FIVE

COUNTRY HOUSES, LOCKED ROOMS AND STEAM TRAINS

1

THE VILLAGE FETE

Miss Chief / Damson jam / Not spoken for 2 years / Luncheon Society

Miss Deeds / Raspberry jam / Not spoken for 5 years / Bridge Society

Miss Lead / Apricot jam / Not spoken for a year / Sewing Society

Miss Place / Strawberry jam / Not spoken for 6 weeks / Gardening Society

Miss Takes / Plum jam / Not spoken for 3 weeks / Craft Society

The murderess is Miss Lead. The raspberry jam (Miss Deeds) is discounted, as is the Luncheon Society lady (Miss Chief). The ladies involved in the 3 and 6 week quarrels are eliminated from the suspects (Miss Takes and Miss Place). Only one suspect remains . . . Miss Lead.

2

TRACKING

Start to station one: Peters and Clarke. Station one to station three: Peters and Noakes. Station three to station four: Peters and Mason. Station four to station five: Mason and Lawrence

Two people are in the carriage as the train sets off. For Peters to travel with everyone except Lawrence, he must either get in at the start and get out at station four, or, he gets in at station one and gets out at station five. Noakes gets in at the first stop (stated) so Peters must be there as the train starts its journey. Lawrence cannot get in at the start and as Mason gets in after Clarke (stated), Clarke and Peters share the carriage from the start. Noakes takes Clarke's place at the first stop. No one boards or exits at station two (stated). At station three Noakes disembarks and Mason boards. Noakes must get out there, or else Peters will not share the carriage with Mason (stated that Lawrence is the only person who doesn't share with Peters). Peters gets out at station four and Lawrence gets in. Mason and Lawrence are the people who arrive at the final station.

3

WHEN THERE'S A WILL . . .

The item inherited is the BANK.

1 Will, **2** Sill, **3** Silk, **4** Sulk, **5** Bulk, **6** Bunk, **7** Bank, **8** Bane, **9** Wane, **10** Wine, **11** Wind, **12** Wild.

4

MALDARK MURDERS

Victim 1: Governess, Library, Poison.
Victim 2: Coachman, Conservatory, Rope.
Victim 3: Groom, Dining Room, Candlestick.
Victim 4: Housekeeper, Pantry, Pistol.

At least two crimes are committed after the governess's murder. As the coachman is the second victim, the governess has to be victim number 1. The groom cannot be fourth as the weapon in that case was a pistol. He was the third victim, making the housekeeper fourth. As poison was used before the murder in the conservatory it can't be to blame for murder number three, so it must have been used on the governess and the coachman was murdered in the conservatory with the rope. As the housekeeper was not murdered in the library the governess must have perished there. Therefore the housekeeper was murdered in the pantry.

MURDERER'S MOVEMENTS:

The murderer turned left in to the library (victim 1). He went in to the inner hall and then the conservatory (victim 2). Moving through the lounge into the hall, he turned left in to the dining room (victim 3). He moved through the kitchen to the pantry (victim 4). From there he went in the storeroom, moved in to the laundry and then left by the side door.

5

AT YOUR SERVICE

Lord Moneybags has 29 servants.

Written out in capitals as TWENTY NINE it contains twenty-nine straight lines.

6

LET OFF STEAM

The journey is: Mouldsy, Murky Bottoms, Hayridge, Lower Lea, Higher Lea, Wrecksem, Topley, Sage Cutting, Leaveham, Outer Thyme, Parsley Hill, Loxley Junction, Down Market, Styx, Up Styx, Crawling, Willbee, Notmuch Appens.

Travelling from Mouldsy to anywhere, you cannot visit all the stations and finish at Lower Lea or Wrecksem.

7

FARE'S FAIR

Whatever the destination, LATE's system was that they charged £1 for every consonant in the name of the destination and £2 for every vowel.

8

HEDGE YOUR BETS

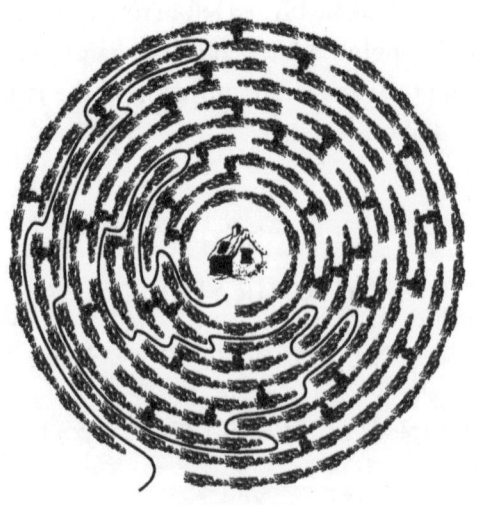

CHAPTER SIX

THE DIABOLICAL MASTERMINDS

1

SOHO SQUARE

Operation Oboe is the name of the latest heist. Nine of the ten words jotted down can be used to complete THREE word squares each with the word SOHO in it. In a word square the four words read the same across and down. There is one word that is unused. That will be the chosen word.

The completed word squares read:

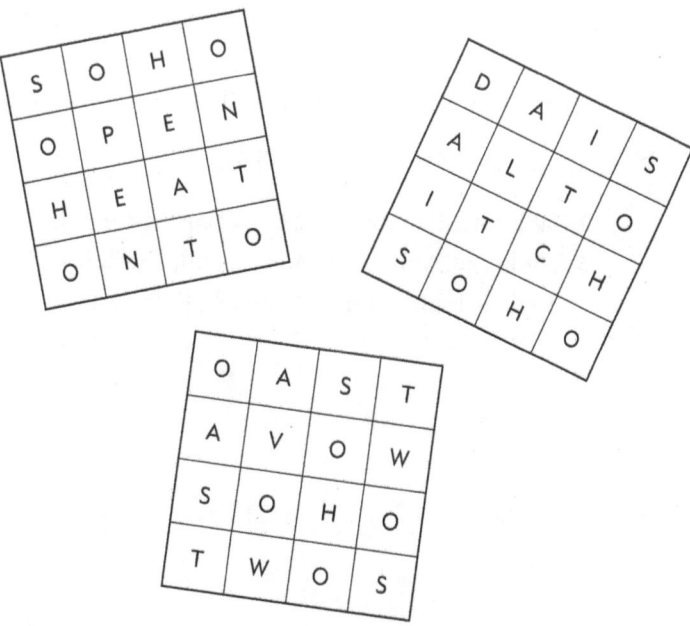

2

ILLUSION CUT DIAMOND

3

THREE WAY SPLIT

1 Banknote, Notebook, **2** Crowbar, Bartender,
3 Goldmine, Minefield, **4** Handcuff, Cufflinks,
5 Jailbird, Birdbath, **6** Sidekick, Kickstart.

4

MISSING JEWELLERY

The DIAMOND is missing.

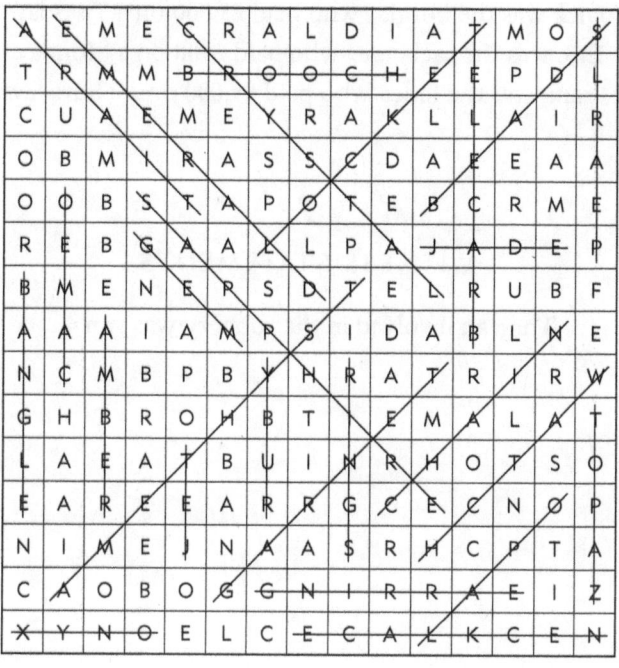

5

MOVING THE MASTERPIECES

1 Degas, Manet, **2** Lowry, Monet, **3** Renoir, Stubbs,
4 Titian, Warhol, **5** Gauguin, Picasso.

The letters in the names of artists have been split up.

6

THE INSPECTOR INVESTIGATES

Bobby was the conman who paid £1,000 on a Friday.
Charlie was the forger who paid £50 on a Wednesday.
Dick was the burglar who paid £3,000 on a Tuesday.
Eric was the racketeer who paid £500 on a Monday.
Frank was the fence who paid £5,000 on a Thursday.

7

WITNESS STATEMENTS

The van involved in the robbery was van 4.

CHAPTER SEVEN

THE HINTERLAND OF HUMAN NATURE

1

DISCARD PILE

Let sleeping dogs lie.

2

JUST THE OPPOSITE

Across: 8 Avarice, 9 Obese, 10 Thick, 11 Overdue, 12 Huge, 13 Hysteria, 16 Numerous, 18 Free, 21 Sincere, 23 Trash, 25 Might, 26 Defrost.

Down: 1 Fact, 2 Daring, 3 Risky, 4 Hero, 5 Honesty, 6 Sender, 7 Relegate, 12 Handsome, 14 You, 15 Cruelty, 17 Manage, 19 Reason, 20 Stiff, 22 Ends, 24 Hits.

3

THE WHOLE TRUTH

Charlotte was in the greenhouse. Donald was in the study. Simon was in the garage. Vanessa was in the kitchen.

Donald has been identified as being in the greenhouse, garage and kitchen. Therefore he has to have been in the place where no one says he was. That is the study. As well as Donald, the second speaker says Charlotte and Vanessa have been in the garage, which means that they haven't been there. That leaves Simon to be in the garage. The third speaker declares that, 'I'm not Charlotte'. As she is lying, that means she is Charlotte. Charlotte was not where she said, the kitchen, leaving only the greenhouse. Vanessa has to have been in the kitchen.

4

CHANCE IT

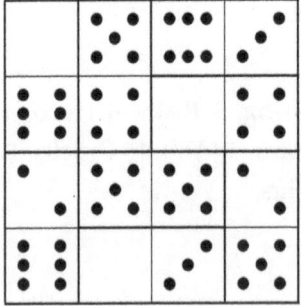

5

LAW AND ORDER

Phase 1: 1 Coffee, 2 Thames, 3 Albums, 4 Friday, 5 Roared, 6 Tennis. Row C spells out FABIAN.

Phase 2: The Anatomy of Crime.

6

INFORMERS

1 H, 2 I, 3 E, 4 D, 5 B, 6 J, 7 C, 8 K, 9 F, 10 A, 11 L, 12 G.

There are 36 pieces of information. (Three people giving x 12 pieces of information.) 21 pieces of information are incorrect. (Three people each placing seven people incorrectly.) It follows that 15 pieces of information must be correct (36 − 21 =15) and that X, Y and Z have each named FIVE people correctly. All information about C is incorrect (stated) and every other individual has been correctly placed at least once (stated). So of the 15 correct places, 11 are accounted for. There is no instance of X, Y and Z all agreeing, but there are FOUR occasions when two people agree. (11 + 4 = 15). E, F, L and G are all verified by two people, so they have to be in the correct positions. Z has placed B incorrectly (stated). X placed B as third to leave, but this cannot be correct as the third person to leave has been identified as E. Therefore Y must be correct with his positioning of B. Y now has already placed FIVE people correctly. His other SEVEN pieces of information have to be incorrect. From now on process of elimination dictates the order. C incorrectly placed by X, Y and Z must occupy the remaining position after the other ELEVEN have been placed. C was the seventh to leave.

7

FORGERY

1, 2, 3, 4 and 6 are fakes.

Signature 5 is the genuine one.

CHAPTER EIGHT

WATCHING THE DETECTIVES

WARNING: SPOILERS AHEAD!

1

MURDERS IN THE RUE MORGUE
by Edgar Allen Poe

The first clue lay in the voices; what was this unknown language? And the bag of gold coins: why did the killer not take them? And why stuff a body up a chimney? Dupin reasoned that the unknown language was not human: it was the vocalising of a primate. The tufts of hair belonged to an orangutan – as, weirdly, did the razor. Dupin made enquiries around the city about any such escaped beast, and at last came to a sailor who had kept it in captivity. The story was fantastical: the ape had watched the sailor shaving; and having escaped, first tried to imitate the man. When the sailor found him loose, the ape fled with the blade; clambered up the lightning rod on the side of the Rue Morgue apartments; climbed into the apartment, tried to 'shave' the older lady but ended up slashing her; and in its panic and rage, strangling her daughter. The sailor caught up with the ape, the ape threw the first body out of the window and stuffed the other up the chimney – before fleeing through the window.

2

THE ADVENTURE OF THE SPECKLED BAND

by Sir Arthur Conan Doyle

Death in this instance is delivered not by hand, but by fang. The ventilator hole in the room is the point of ingress for the deadly assailant. The bell cord is not connected because the victim must not get the chance to ring for help before the poison has taken its course. And 'the speckled band' is the most chilling of metaphorical images: the 'band' being a venomous tropical snake, an 'Indian swamp adder' (there is no such thing), induced to slither through the ventilation and discovered, once the candle is lit, wrapped around that useless bell cord, waiting to bite . . . But as Holmes and Watson find, that which can be persuaded to slither in can equally be persuaded to slither out again, to strike in the room of the perpetrator . . .

3

THE CASE OF THE CONSTANT SUICIDES

by John Dickson Carr

The twists and turns in this yarn are as abrupt as a wild fairground ride. The collapsible wire animal cage gives rise to the suspicion that this is a mystery involving an animal – but the only creature here is a red herring. While characters speculate about victims being terrified enough by raging beasts to jump through windows, the truth lies in a suicide made to look like murder, and an attempted murder made to look like attempted suicide: the room is locked by means of a device poked through wire mesh, and the deadly agent is not an animal, but a form of toxic gas that induces disorientation and panic, and which dissipates quickly through an open window – all in the services of the twisty-minded villain who is anxious to get hold of an inheritance . . .

4

THE BIG BOW MYSTERY

by Israel Zangwill

Indeed, the solution to the ghastly mystery is not just about time; it is about a matter of seconds. And a lethal sleight of hand. Remember, the locked door had been forced open by both the landlady and the retired detective, and then the retired detective examined the corpse while she momentarily held back. Except it wasn't a corpse the detective was examining . . . Arthur Constant was in a deep sleep thanks to the draught given to him the night before by the detective. His murderer was in fact the detective, who slashed the sleeping man's throat with impressive speed, as the landlady was still fearfully hanging back for a few minutes. The fatal blade went straight back into the pocket of the detective, who then continued his 'examination'. The motive for this horror? The retired detective wanted to see the world through a killer's eyes: and devise a murder like an artwork.

5

THE MYSTERY OF THE YELLOW ROOM

by Gaston Leroux

The key to the mystery lies in the question of who can be trusted; the vanishing assassin is not a ghost, but a man known to the daughter of the house, the same daughter aids his 'disappearance' as the others race around. But what of the attempt upon her life within that locked Yellow Room? Again, she knows her assailant; and while there was violence, it did not happen as she claimed. Indeed, she was always alone in that room. There was a struggle with her assailant earlier in the day; but the cause of the horrible injury to her temple was when later that night she fell out of bed and hit her head against the sharp side of the table. This is a house of dark personal secrets; and an invisible assassin is a preferable story to that of mental distress and hidden scandal . . .

6

THE ABSENCE OF MR GLASS

by G.K. Chesterton

The sinister Mr Glass has not vanished into thin air; because the sinister Mr Glass never existed in the first place. The idea of his existence had in fact been the result of a simple and comical mis-hearing. What Maggie did not know about her fiancé James is that behind the locked door, he was secretly practising a stage magician act and didn't want anyone to know until he had perfected it. That is the reason for the top hat; it is Todhunter's. And the smashed whiskey tumblers? They indeed are Mr Glass. For Todhunter had been practising juggling them and when they were dropped, crossly exclaimed 'Missed a glass.'

7

SO LONG AT THE FAIR

by Anthony Thorne

This tantalising mystery involves a most strenuous conspiracy but unusually, it is all in the public interest. At first this existential nightmare touches on questions of sanity; but all is restored with a simple count of the balconies. Outside the hotel, on the floor with the 'vanished' room, there are six balconies; but inside, there are only five rooms. Why the extra balcony? Because one room has been sealed off; the room in which the brother was sleeping. The hotel owners reveal that they were in collaboration with the authorities; the brother Johnny – who was so tired - was in fact carrying a form of the plague. He is now in hospital, but his existence, and indeed the existence of the room itself, had to be denied because the authorities were terrified of starting a plague panic at the time of the Great Exhibition. Brother and sister are at last reunited.

8

THE MIRACLE OF MOON CRESCENT

by G.K. Chesterton

One of Father Brown's more sinister mysteries, this locked room enigma is based both on simple psychology and on the reversal of expectations. When the gunshot goes off in the street below, millionaire Warren Wynd does what anyone would do; he pokes his head out of the window to see what is going on. That is the moment his fate is sealed. The gunshot was a trap, and from a floor above, a noose is dropped down over Wynd's neck. The strong man holding it yanks the man out of the window. Wynd does not fall, as Father Brown observes; rather, he rises. Hauled upwards, he is strangled by the coils; and then his body is lowered to an accomplice in the park, who arranges the dangling corpse on the tree. The aim of the killer was not financial, but vengeance for a decades-old slight; and in such a way to make it seem that supernatural forces had creepily taken him from the room and hung him from the tree.

9

THE NAME OF THE ROSE

by Umberto Eco

In this, the most absurdly and delightfully erudite whodunnit, Brother William of Baskerville sees a range of possibilities in every clue, from the theology and symbolism of the Apocalypse to the architecture of ancient libraries; for this reason, he is for a time stumped by the locked room and the mirror and the message. But 'the first and seventh of the four' is a mis-reading: it is supposed to be 'the first and the seventh of quatuor' (the word quatuor meaning quartet or four); by pressing the first and seventh letters above the door, he releases a hidden hinge mechanism. The mirror is a door. But what lies within that locked room is lethal: a much sought-after ancient book, written out on papyrus and cloth, thought lost to the world forever. Anyone leafing through it dies agonisingly . . . because a murderous monk has coated those pages with a poison that they absorb when licking their fingers to turn the pages . . . And his motivation? Without giving away the title of the book, this medieval murderer is desperate to prevent comedy and laughter becoming permissible and indeed celebrated by holy men; he believes that laughter reduces men to apes . . .

10

CRIME IN NOBODY'S ROOM

by John Dickson Carr

Here is a locked room mystery from a bad dream; the innocent party unlocking a door to discover a familiar world turned uncanny and evil. And how can this flat then no longer exist? Eccentric Colonel March is on the trail. Young Ronald Denham was – despite the different furnishings – in his own flat. But earlier that evening, while he was out enjoying his boozy excess, the killer got into his flat via the fire-escape, and as planned, redecorated it with new pictures, lamps and ornaments. He had lured his victim there under the guise of a business meeting and needed the place to not seem familiar. But Denham got home a shade earlier than anticipated so the killer knocked him out to cover his tracks, while also carefully removing the body, plus all traces of the counterfeit decorations. But Colonel March discovers that the killer, who lured his victim to the block posing as the block's well-to-do owner, was colour-blind and could not see that he had put the corpse's coat on inside out. And that a reproduction of an Old Master he had hung upon the wall actually had no colours at all but sepia. The whole affair was an elaborate financial swindle.

CHAPTER NINE

FOOTSTEPS IN THE FOG

1

MIND YOUR MANORS

2D.

2

BLOCKS

Words Across: FOG, ICE, TENS, ARE, NEW

Words Down: FIT, OCEAN, GENRE, SEW.

3

A STEP AT A TIME

1 The steps are:
TENTH, TENCH, TEACH, PEACH, PEACE, PLACE.

2 The steps are:
SWORD, SWORE, SHORE, CHORE, CHOSE, CHASE.

4

NO HIDING PLACE

The words above are anagrams which when unravelled read: Singer, Painter, Artist, Dancer, Designer, Organist, Orchestra. The fugitive is hiding in a theatre.

5

LETSBY AVENUE

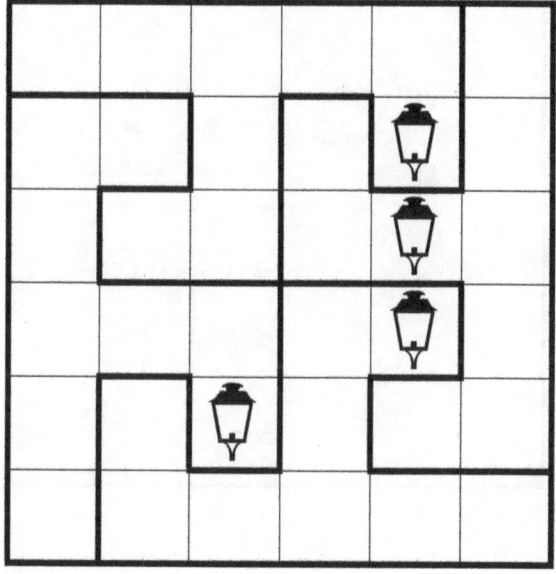

6

ONE WAY SYSTEM

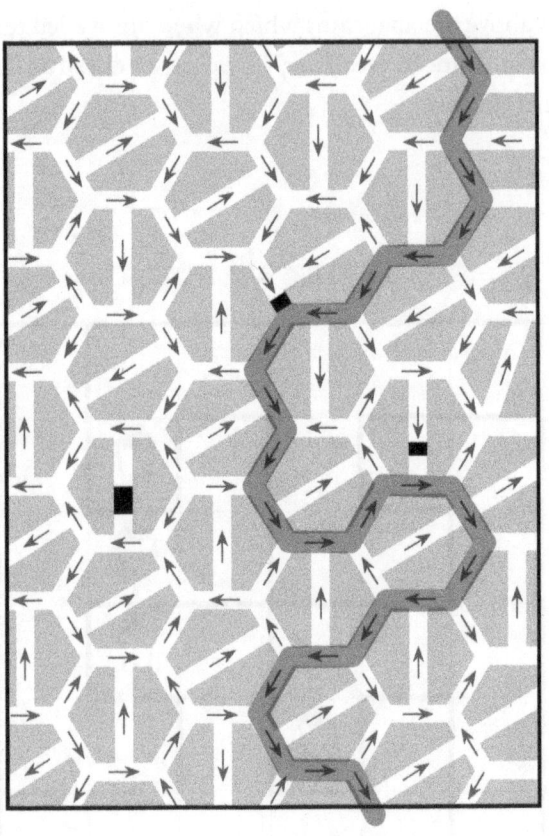

7

PAWNBROKER

The answer is 1991. The other tickets read the same when you turn the tickets upside down.

CHAPTER TEN

THE GLOBAL ARM OF THE LAW

1

CAPITAL OFFENCE

1 Oslo, 2 Seoul, 3 Brussels, 4 Colombo, 5 Rome.

1 = O, 2 = S, 3 = L, 4 = E,
5 = U, 6 = B, 7 = R, 8 = C, 9 = M.

2

WHERE TO?

EIGHT countries have been investigated. The names are revealed by joining words or parts of words together. Each sentence contains a country. In order they are: Germany, Malta, Chile, China, Lebanon, Iran, Argentina and India.

3

INTERPOL'S INTERCEPTION

The answer is b) Secret documents are to be destroyed at once! The sentences in the message begin with Ja, Fe, Ma, Ap, Ma, Ju, Ju and Au, i.e. the months from January to August. The next in sequence must be Se (for September) so b) is correct.

4

SAIL AWAY

Yacht number 4. The same design elements appear in the sails and on the body of the boat for the first three meetings. The difference is the order of patterns. At Monaco, the sail designs starting top left and moving clockwise feature black circle on white, white, black and black stripes. The top sail is the same as the top left of the main sails. The body of the boat is the same as the sail layout. In Nice the yacht had the same design arrangement, but the different elements move a space clockwise. Top sail and body follow the main sail pattern. Again, in the Bay of Naples, the various elements move clockwise once again. Following this established pattern, the yacht at Saint-Tropez will have white top left area of the main sail. Moving in a clockwise direction, top right sail is black, lower right sail is striped and lower left is white with a black circle. The top sail is white. The body of the boat follows the pattern of the sails.

5

MOVING ON

The word order is: Holland, Austria, Finland, Belgium, Iceland, Denmark, Germany. The eighth country, reading diagonally from top left to lower right, is HUNGARY.

6

INTERLOCKING

The three-letter words are either letters 1, 3 and 5, or 2, 4 and 6 of the six-letter words. The words you make are as follows: ALLIED, LOUNGE, PAINED and SWEATS. These words are made from ALE and LID, LUG and ONE, PIE and AND and finally SET and WAS.

The initial letters spell out ALPS so you are heading for those mountains.

CHAPTER ELEVEN

THE YARD IN THE FUTURE

1

BLUES IN TWOS

1 Antiquarian, **2** Sheepish, **3** Terminate, **4** Steadfast, **5** Enlighten, **6** Esplanades, **7** Keepsake, **8** Thirtieth, **9** Originator, **10** Recapture.

2

FOLLOWING ORDERS

The opening letter of each sentence moves forward in alphabetical order. Logically, a letter K will indicate the meeting place. In each sentence there is a number starting with twelve and working down. The number is written as a word and the name of the number may be split between words. Logically the meeting will be at 2 p.m. at King's Cross Station.

3

SWIPE CARD

The key will open room 22.

1 ←⋯, 2 ⋯→, 3 ↔, 4 ↕, 5 ↕, 6 ⤢, 7 ↓.

4

THE POWER OF OBSERVATION

5

DOWNLOAD THE APP

All the missing words contain the letters app in that order.

1 Applause, clapped, rapport, approached, tapping, swapped.
2 Appeared, sapphires, wrapped, disappeared, appeal, strapped, apprehended, happen.
3 Chappie, happy, appetite, apples, pineapples, approval, snapped, approach.

6

KEYPAD

The message reads: I can see you on the jetty if you want. Is noon tomorrow OK? I hope so.

7

THE PERFECT PASSCODE

572136489

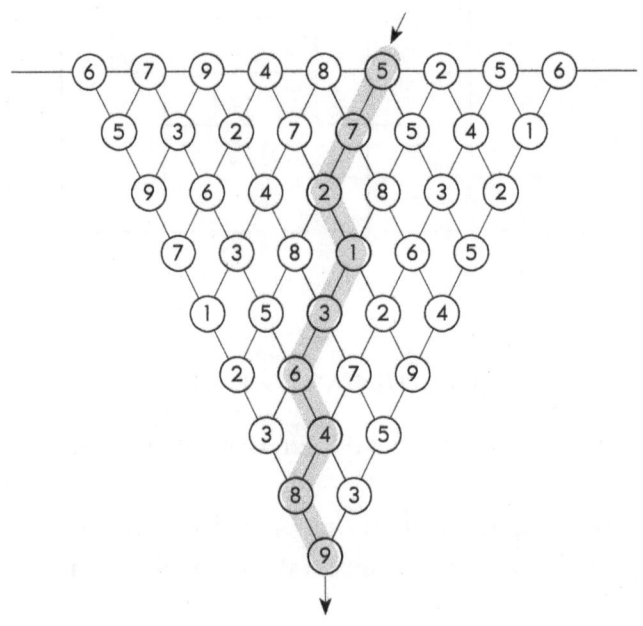

CHAPTER TWELVE

THE FINAL CHALLENGE

Note: Strictly speaking – as with many questions to do with the law, and justice, and human nature – there can be subtly different interpretations of different circumstances. The answers below are the considered overviews of the 1930s examiners overseeing the tests and in that sense they point out the salient points of each case, but are not completely definitive. These answers highlight what the correct procedure should have been; and raise when some of the candidates either went too far, or not far enough. Whether it is pub licensing laws (rather stricter in the 1930s for landlords and drinkers alike!) or espionage, these considered answers and opinions shine a light into the legal minds of a distant era . . .

QUESTION 1:

'A number of candidates made no effort to detain the man and confront him with the ladies; others charged the offender with taking upon himself the designation of a police officer without making any enquiry as to ascertain whether or not he was a Metropolitan police officer. A few candidates, in order, as they thought, to give themselves the power of arrest for assault or insulting behaviour, went beyond the scope of the question by stating that they had actually witnessed the man accost the ladies and seize one of them by the arm.'

QUESTION 2:

'Several candidates placed the responsibility for dealing with the man upon the Relieving Officer, while others called the Divisional Surgeon to ascertain whether it was a case of illness, in spite of the history of the case and the evidence available to them. A number of candidates were also hazy as to whose responsibility it was to bring the man before a Justice in Lunacy within three days.'

QUESTION 3:

'Reviewing the answers to this question, it is clear that many officers did not know the difference between a "Dying Deposition" and "Dying Declaration". In the first case the correct action was to arrange for the taking of a "Dying Deposition" by acquainting the Clerk of the Court at which the prisoners had appeared so that a Court could be convened at the bedside of the dying woman and her evidence taken on oath by a magistrate . . .

The second case necessitated the taking of a "Dying Declaration". Such declarations are only taken in cases of suspected murder or manslaughter, either by a Magistrate or if not available, a senior police officer, in the presence of a doctor.'

QUESTION 4:

'Although the question was quite clear as to permitted hours, several candidates confused their answers by taking into consideration the supper house extension'.

QUESTION 5:

'Obtain the names and addresses of the boys in case they abscond; also their ages. Obtain the name and address of the lady and inspect her driving licence and insurance. Take particulars of the car and point out the offence of leaving the engine running. Report the lady for process, or give her a verbal warning. In the presence of the boys, question the lady as to whether she gave permission for the boys to get into and drive the vehicle. Ask her whether she is willing to assist the police and to prefer a charge. Request her to attend the station . . . Arrest the boys and take them to the station by police van where they should be charged with "being concerned together with taking and driving away a motor vehicle without the owner's consent". The Station Officer will arrange for the youths' parents to be informed . . . The boy who drove the car should be charged with driving without insurance and, if under 17, further charged with driving while disqualified by reason of age.'

QUESTION 6:

'The Duty Officer should obtain the names and addresses of both witnesses, take statements from them and request them to attend the station. The ladies should be asked to make a note of the index (registration) number and of the description of the car and occupants . . . the name and address of the doctor should also be obtained. CID should be informed and steps taken to ensure the body is not removed . . . the Duty Officer should proceed to note any marks on the roadway, broken glass and other parts of the car which may have been left at the scene . . . At the garage of the owner of the car an examination should be carried out by the Duty Officer for clues. The owner should be requested not to enter his garage until CID have attended. The duty officer should make enquiries in the vicinity regarding the suspects and obtain from the owner a full description of his car . . . (the car) is to be preserved for fingerprints when found. The Duty Officer should obtain a full description of the deceased . . . details may be published in the Police Gazette. If the deceased is not identified quickly, arrangements should be made for the body to be photographed and fingerprinted.'

QUESTION 7:

'The following offences have been committed: (i) Forgery (Section 2, Forgery Act 1913); (ii) Uttering a forged document (Section 6, Forgery Act 1913); (iii) Obtaining on a forged instrument (Section 7, Forgery Act 1913); (iv) Stealing the cheque book; (v) Receiving the cheque. The officer in charge of the case should: (i) Enquire at Cheque Index, Central Registry Office, to obtain particulars of cheque book (if registered) and to link up other offences which may have been committed with other cheques; (ii) If cheque book is not registered in Cheque Index, enquire at bank and of loser of book to obtain particulars and cause them to be registered at CRO; (iii) Enquire at CRO to establish identity of wanted man; (iv) Take tradesman to CRO to view albums (photographs) to endeavour to establish the identity of the wanted man; (v) Cause particulars to be circulated in the Police Gazette.'

QUESTION 8:

'This question was answered by 15 candidates, all of whom were CID officers. No definite answer was laid down by the examiners, each paper being marked on its merits. The following will show briefly the kind of action required under such circumstances: (i) Before moving the body or allowing anything to be disturbed, cause photographs to be taken from many angles in all parts of the house; (ii) Mention to the pathologist the necessity for taking specimens of digested and undigested food in order that the last meals and the time of death can be narrowed down; (iii) Also ask the pathologist to examine microscopically the material beneath the victim's fingernails, as she might have made some attempt to defend herself by scratching; (iv) Specimens of dust and fibres from the carpet and hair from the victim to be taken for comparisons with specimens to be taken from the suspect's clothing when located; (v) Obtain from the pathologist an accurate measurement of the penetrating wound . . . ; (vi) There being no marks of forced entry, it is possible that the murderer was known to the victim and freely admitted into the house or was lawfully in possession of the key. The contents of all rooms and all correspondence, visiting cards, address books to be carefully examined. All persons indicated in this discovery to be interrogated and asked to account for their movements; (vii) The murderer might have been a strolling chance thief who slipped in while the front door was left open unattended . . . arrange a house to house enquiry . . . to ascertain descriptions of any suspicious caller or loiterer . . . ascertain whether anyone had missed a hammer or discovered a bloodstained hammer; (viii) Another special enquiry at all tool shops in the neighbourhood to trace the recent purchase of a hammer; (ix) All known thieves, especially those known to resort to violence . . . to be called upon to account for their movements. Their clothing is to be examined for bloodstains; (x) Postmen, refuse collectors, beggars, pedlars and local epileptic sufferers to receive attention; (xi) In view of the fact that no-one was seen to enter or leave the house, endeavour, when the person most likely to be the murderer is traced, to obtain from him a statement as to his movements on the day of the crime.'

QUESTION 9:

'Many candidates dealt with the question of the postcards being obscene, describing the test of obscenity. A number of candidates arrested and charged the seller without any evidence of the sale or offering for sale of these obscene prints. The answer to the question turned chiefly on the power of arrest. 'Mr C''s name and address should first have been noted. If he desired to charge without any further action it should have been pointed out to him that the evidence was very meagre. The best course would have been to have induced 'Mr C' to purchase an obscene postcard. The transaction having been witnessed by you, sufficient evidence would have been provided to justify arrest.'

QUESTION 10

'The points in this case were as follows: 'Mr A' insisted on charging. The alleged assault occurred on the premises of the injured man. The passage was unlighted. There was an admitted struggle. It was word against word. The provocation was apparent owing to the alleged enticing away of the wife. The parties were well known to each other. A husband is entitled to make enquiries in order to trace his wife. The passage was dark so doubt would exist as to whether 'Mrs B' could have witnessed the struggle and alleged assault. Doubt might exist as to whether there had in fact been an assault owing to a struggle having taken place. 'Mr B' was quite quiet and was likely to be amenable to reason.

The general procedure regarding cases of this kind is that where there is corroborative evidence of wounds or injury, and the police have good reason to believe that a serious assault has been committed recently although not within their view, they are justified in taking into custody the person charged by some other with having committed an assault occasioning actual bodily harm . . . There was a good deal of confusion on the question of whether 'Mrs B' could give evidence against her husband. The general rule is as follows: At Common Law, the husband or wife of a defendant is not a competent witness for the Crown against the defendant.'

QUESTION 11:

'A person who frightens another person to death may be guilty of murder or manslaughter just as if he had used other means to accelerate death. If evidence can be obtained to show that 'M' knew of Mrs 'P''s state of health, or if it can be inferred that 'M' intended to carry out his threat, and that the result would probably have caused Mrs 'P''s death or inflicted grievous bodily harm on her, it would be murder. If no such evidence is available and no such inference can be drawn, then it is manslaughter and this is probably what a jury would find.'

QUESTION 12:

'He has committed an offence against Section 1 The Official Secrets Act 1911, viz: "for a purpose prejudicial to the safety or interests of the State obtaining information . . . which was calculated to be, or might have been, or was intended to be directly or indirectly useful to the enemy." The effect of the finding of the diary in X's possession is . . . to place upon the accused the onus of proving that he did NOT obtain the documents for a purpose prejudicial to the safety or interest of the State.

The action to be taken once the document was found in 'Mr X''s possession would be to caution him, arrest him and take him to the nearest police station. A statement should be obtained from an officer of Military Intelligence who should be in a position to give evidence that the name and address found in the diary were those of a foreign agent. If the diary has been found in the house of the accused and not upon his person, then it would be necessary to give evidence of his constructive possession to prove that the name and address of the foreign agent shown therein was in 'Mr X''s own handwriting.'

QUESTION 13:

'Very few officers attempted this question and of those who did, ninety per cent suggested that the offences committed were either Common Assault, Indecent Assault or the Road Traffic offences of "failing to stop after an accident" and failing to report an accident.

They failed to appreciate that there was no accident. The action of the driver in refusing to stop to allow his passenger to alight was deliberate, as also was the action of the young woman who jumped out of the car while it was in motion.

The offence disclosed was causing "Grievous Bodily Harm" contrary to section 18, or "Malicious Wounding" contrary to section 20 of the Offences Against the Person Act, 1861.

If the driver could be traced within a few hours of the crime he could have been arrested and charged under Section 18, but if not a warrant could be obtained under Section 20.

This question was based on facts and the defendant was convicted of "malicious wounding", heavily fined and ordered to pay substantial costs.'

QUESTION 14:

(i) Locality: Hampton (the sign on the post office); Date: April 11 (the morning after the dance); Time: 4.40 a.m.

(ii) Next door premises: Barclays Bank

(iii) The vehicle was on Oxley Road; the business was 'Green Brook Steam Laundry'

(iv) The dance was held in the upstairs ballroom of the Crown Hotel

(v) Yes, there were two people in the vehicle; registration plate AOY 19

ACKNOWLEDGEMENTS

It is time for one final flourish of the magnifying glass: to detect the diabolical geniuses who were key to this criminal cornucopia of puzzles and enigmas. Huge thanks to Dr Clare Smith, manager of the Metropolitan Police Heritage Centre, and guardian of its archive, who expertly set me on the trail of many historical mysteries; also to the dazzlingly fiendish masterminds Roy and Sue Preston who devised and set the ingenious puzzles. Thanks to copyeditor Sophie Lazar, and proofreader Sally Sargeant, whose keen eyes could open a safe from a 100 yards, and of course, thanks to top publicist Jessica Farrugia and marketing guru Vicky Abbott, for getting the word out on to the street. Lastly, thanks to Katie Packer, with her formidable forensic skills; my agent Anna Power, who knows where all the bodies are buried; and Sarah Emsley, the ringleader, and brains of the entire operation.

Discover more ingenious brainteasers from bestselling author
Sinclair McKay to put your mind to the test . . .

Could you have outsmarted an Enigma machine?

The Bletchley Park recruiters left no stone unturned when
searching for the best code breakers in the land. To assess
the individuals they found they devised various ingenious
mind-twisters – hidden codes, cryptic crosswords, secret
languages, complex riddles – and it is puzzles like these,
together with the fascinating recruitment stories that
surround them, that make up this book.

Would Bletchley Park have recruited YOU?

All Sinclair McKay's books are available
in paperback and as ebooks

Pit your wits against the minds of our time.

Weaving astonishing stories of the men and women who
operate from the shadows, the secret heroes and heroines
of MI5 and MI6 who have faced extraordinary and terrifying
challenges, and a wide range of mind-boggling puzzles, *Secret
Service Brainteasers* will test your mental agility to discover:

Do YOU have what it takes to be a spy?